CRIME AND THE NATIVE AMERICAN

CRIME AND THE NATIVE AMERICAN

By

DAVID LESTER, Ph.D.

Professor of Psychology
Richard Stockton State College
Pomona, New Jersey

Charles C Thomas
PUBLISHER • LTD.
SPRINGFIELD • ILLINOIS • U.S.A.

Published and Distributed Throughout the World by

CHARLES C THOMAS · PUBLISHER, LTD.
2600 South First Street
Springfield, Illinois 62794-9265

© *1999 by* CHARLES C THOMAS · PUBLISHER, LTD.

ISBN 0-398-06983-2 (cloth)
ISBN 0-398-06984-0 (paper)

Library of Congress Catalog Card Number: 99-31537

Printed in the United States of America
CR-R-3

Library of Congress Cataloging in Publication Data

Lester, David, 1942-
    Crime and the Native American / by David Lester.
        p.   cm.
    Includes bibliographical references and index.
    ISBN 0-398-06983-2 (cloth). -- ISBN 0-398-06984-0 (pbk.)
    1. Indians of North America--Social conditions. 2. Crime--United
States. 3. Criminal justice, Administration of--United States.
I. Title.
E98.C87L47   1999
364.3'497--dc21   99-31537
                                                                    CIP

PREFACE

It is believed that Native Americans have a high frequency of criminal behavior and, in addition, are subjected to great discrimination by the criminal justice system, as are other minority groups. The present book explores the data and research that has been conducted on criminal behavior in Native Americans in order to see whether these beliefs are indeed valid.

Although a number of articles have appeared in scholarly journals on criminal behavior in Native Americans, only two books have appeared on the topic (both cited in the present book), and both of these were edited books. Edited books have the disadvantage of lacking both comprehensiveness and a coherent and coordinated presentation. This book is the first by a single author on the topic of criminal behavior in general in Native Americans.

To prepare this book, I searched out and read all published articles on criminal behavior in Native Americans. Some material on Native Canadians is included as well since Native North Americans do not necessarily divide into two distinct groups based on the division of the land by the United States and Canada. However, the two criminal justice systems are quite different, and so conclusions from research on the criminal justice system in one of the nations may not generalize to the other.

The literature review is not comprehensive for criminal behavior in Native Canadians. There was some difficulty in obtaining sound research studies on criminal behavior in Native Canadians because many of the publications were government documents. Government documents do not always meet the criteria for sound research and have not undergone peer review as have articles published in scholarly journals.

Although much has been written about criminal behavior in Native Americans, this survey found that many writers make little effort to support their opinions with research studies. Furthermore, some of the research has been methodologically poor. For example, estimates of the incidence of criminal behavior in Native Americans have made no attempt to control for the age structure of Native Americans (the Native American population is younger than the general population) or their lower socioeconomic status.

In addition to reviewing what is known about criminal behavior in Native Americans, this book identifies issues and topics which have been neglected and errors in previous research which must be corrected in future studies. It is hoped, therefore, that this book will stimulate further studies on criminal behavior in Native Americans.

D.L.

CONTENTS

Page

Preface   v

Chapter

PART 1–INTRODUCTION

1.   Introduction   5
2.   The personal and social conditions of Native Americans   13
3.   The frequency of Native American crime   23
4.   Alcohol and crime   41

PART 2–CRIMES AND MISDEMEANORS

5.   Murder   53
6.   Child abuse and neglect   66
7.   Other criminal behaviors   78

PART 3–THEORIES OF NATIVE AMERICAN CRIMINAL BEHAVIOR

8.   General theories   87
9.   Positivist individualistic theories   97
10.   Social structure theories   102
11.   Social process theories   109

PART 4–THE CRIMINAL JUSTICE SYSTEM

12.   Native American policing   123
13.   The law and the courts   132
14.   Prisons and probation   140
15.   Discrimination in the criminal justice system   154

PART 5–CONCLUSIONS

16.   Conclusion   171

Appendix: Tables   175
Index   183

CRIME AND THE NATIVE AMERICAN

Part 1

INTRODUCTION

Chapter 1

INTRODUCTION

The problem of crime in Native Americans should be of concern to public policymakers for two reasons. The first is that it is claimed that criminal behavior is more common in Native Americans than in the rest of the population. If this were to be true, then effort should be expended to prevent crime in this group. To place this problem in a broader context, it is important to note that other nations have apparently experienced similarly high crime rates in their aboriginal groups, including Australia and Canada (Frideres and Robertson, 1994).

Secondly, the long history of oppression of the Native American by the dominant culture has led to concern among policymakers about the present welfare of Native Americans. The government has several agencies concerned with Native Americans (including the Indian Health Service and the Bureau of Indian Affairs), and the existence of these agencies reflects the concern of the society with the social and personal conditions of Native Americans. In this context, a high crime rate in Native Americans would be an area of special concern.

This book is designed to review what we know at the present time about crime in Native Americans, whether Native Americans are discriminated against by the criminal justice system, and how crime might be prevented in Native Americans. It focuses on the results of empirical research and suggests areas which need further empirical exploration.

Before beginning our review of crime in Native Americans, it will be useful to review briefly the history of Native Americans.

The Demographic History of Native Americans

Native Americans are genetically similar to Asian Mongoloids and arrived from Asia, probably crossing from Siberia to Alaska in several migratory waves from 10,000 to 40,000 years ago. Estimates of the aboriginal population of North America in 1492 A.D. range from 900,000 (Kroeber, 1939) to 18 million (Dobyns, 1983). Thornton (1987) suggests five million for the United States and two million for Canada (out of a world population of about 330 million to 540 million). Estimates of their life expectancy back then range from 19 to 43.

The Native American population decreased from 5 million to about 250,000 in 1900 for several reasons (Thornton, 1987; Snipp, 1992).

(1) An increased death rate due to diseases brought by European settlers, such as smallpox, measles, cholera, diphtheria, and pneumonia.

(2) Warfare and genocide, particularly for some tribes such as the Cherokee.

(3) Removal and relocation from one geographic area to another, especially after the Indian Removal Act of 1830, with high death rates in transit.

(4) Relocation which often split tribes, so that, for example, the Seminole are to be found in Florida and Oklahoma; and combination of tribes that were unrelated, such as the Shoshoni and Arapaho on the Wind River Reservation in Wyoming.

(5) European influences (particularly from missionaries) which destroyed Native American ways of life.

(6) The destruction of their environment, especially the buffalo (from 60 million in aboriginal times to less than 1,000 by 1900) which hastened the social and cultural collapse.

(7) A decrease in fertility as a result of the new diseases, forced migrations, and intermixture with European mates.

The Reservation System

The isolation and concentration of Native Americans began quite early but was legally justified by the Indian Removal Act of 1830. After passage of this act, many tribes located east of the Mississippi River were relocated to the west of the river. The Iroquois (Seneca), for example, were moved from New York to Oklahoma. Those tribes which did not move, such as the Ojibway in Wisconsin, had much of their territory confiscated (Snipp, 1992).

As the Anglo population migrated westwards, the tribes west of the Mississippi River were forced to give up much of the land that had been granted to them, both those native to the region such as the Sioux, and those newly moved there such as the Cherokee. The reservations were often situated on the least desirable land, with few natural resources, and far removed from major urban areas.

The policy then changed toward forcing the Native Americans to assimilate, and the Dawes Act of 1887 permitted the land controlled by Native Americans to be split into small parcels and given to individual Native Americans, with the aim of turning them into ranchers and farmers. In 1953, legislation was passed to remove reservations from their status as independent political entities and to start employment and relocation programs to encourage Native Americans to leave reservations for other parts of the United States. This approach was soon abandoned. However, whereas in 1930 only 10 percent of Native Americans lived in urban areas, by 1970 this percentage had risen to 48 percent (Gundlach et al., 1977). Some 20 percent of Native Americans in 1970 claimed no tribal identity and more than a third of Native American men had married white wives as compared to only 2 percent of African American men.

After 1950, the proportion of Native Americans living on reservations declined from roughly 50 percent to about 25 percent by 1980. In 1980, 336,384 Native Americans lived on reservations and about 14 percent of all Native Americans lived on reservations with poverty rates of 40 percent or more (Sandefur, 1989). Sandefur identified ten reservations with poverty rates of 40 percent or higher and female headship rates of 30 percent or higher, and a further eight reservations with poverty rates of 40 percent or higher but female headship rates of less than 30 percent. Eighteen of the 36 largest reservations (that is, with populations over 2,000) met the criteria for being "underclass," that segment of the poor whose situation seems relatively immune to economic conditions and social programs designed to help.

To counter this poverty, programs exist to educate the youth so that they can more easily move into the mainstream society, and efforts are being made to develop the economies on the reservation through the exploitation of natural resources or the establishment of businesses, such as casinos.

Although there is much to criticize about conditions on the reservations,[1] many Native Americans are content to remain there, for the

---

1. Indeed, Mikel (1980) calls the reservations "concentration camps," and the Bureau of Indian Affairs has been rightfully labeled "The worst federal agency" (Satchell, 1994).

reservations do permit the maintenance of a cultural base for the tribes, where the native language can be spoken and traditional ways followed. There is a strong sense of family and community, and social services are provided on the reservations administered by the tribal governments.

The Twentieth Century

The Native American population has grown during this century, particularly since 1950. Thornton (1987) gives the following numbers:

1890	248,253
1900	237,196
1910	276,927
1920	244,437
1930	343,352
1940	345,252
1950	357,499
1960	523,591
1970	792,730
1980	1,366,676

The reasons for this increase in recent years include;

(1) A high birth rate. The birth rate for Native Americans peaked in 1964 at 43 per 1,000 people. In 1971 it was 33 as compared to a rate of 18 in the United States as a whole. The number of children ever born to 1,000 women aged 15 to 44 was 1687 for Native American women in 1980 as compared to 1302 for the United States as a whole.

(2) The declining death rate among Native Americans. In 1980 the death rate was 5.0 per 1,000 for Native Americans as compared to 8.7 for the United States as a whole. (The infant mortality rate, however, has been higher for Native Americans than for the United States as a whole, though the difference has been decreasing in recent years.)

(3) Changes in the definition and enumeration of Native Americans. Prior to 1960, census observers noted whether they believed a person to be an Native American or not. Since 1960, self-reporting has been used. Many Native American tribes now set criteria for defining a member. For example, the Cherokee Nation of Oklahoma in its constitution developed in the 1970s set no minimum blood quantity for tribal membership. One must merely trace one's descent along Cherokee lines.

Simmons (1977) has listed six ways in which Native Americans may be defined: (1) *legal definitions*, such as being a member of a tribe, (2) *self-declaration*, (3) *community recognition* by other Native Americans, (4) *recognition by non-Native Americans*, (5) *biological definitions*, such as blood mixture, and (6) *cultural definitions*, such as behaving as Native Americans do.

Urbanization

Since 1950, there has been a large-scale movement of Native Americans to urban areas. Thornton (1987) has provided estimates of the percentage of urbanized Native Americans:

1890	0.0%
1900	0.4%
1910	4.5%
1920	6.1%
1930	9.9%
1940	7.2%
1950	13.4%
1960	27.9%
1970	44.5%
1980	49.0%

This urbanization has had three consequences: a declining birth rate among the urban Native Americans, more intermarriage, and reduced tribal importance. In 1980, over half of all Native Americans were married to non-Native Americans as compared to about one percent of whites and two percent of blacks. Thus, in the future, genetic definitions of who is an Native American may make less sense than definition in terms of descent.

Canada

The situation of Native Canadians is perhaps even worse than that of Native Americans. Ward et al. (1978) and Kirmayer (1994) have documented their situation with some striking statistics. By 1994 there were 596 bands of Native Canadians in Canada with access to 2,284 reserves. The average size of the band has grown from about 200 to about 500. In the 1970s about 70 percent of status Native Canadians lived on the reserves, and they numbered about 300,000. In addition, non-status Native Canadians, or Métis, (most of whom have married non-Native Canadians) numbered about 600,000. In addition, there are some 17,000 Eskimos, although they prefer the label "Inuit." Four hundred years ago, there were perhaps about 250,000 Native Canadians. By the beginning of this century, the number was down to about 100,000, but the number rose to about one million by the 1970s.

The birth rate of Native Canadians is higher and the life expectancy lower than for white Canadians. Education is poor and illiteracy common. Housing for status Native Canadians is poor—crowded and often without adequate water and sewage facilities.

Ward characterized the Canadian government policy as a plan to absorb the Native Canadian culture into the dominant white culture. The government was paternalistic, although well-meaning, but left Native Canadians out of the planning for their lives. The reserve system isolated them from the dominant culture, yet the laws restricted their traditional life-style and the social service system impaired their motivation and self-concept. Their language, customs, knowledge and religion were mocked. The Native Canadian could stay on the reservation, face unemployment and the lack of a meaningful life, or migrate to the slums of the cities where they would face racial discrimination and unemployment. Ward noted that it is an indictment of the reservation system that so many Native Canadians chose the city slums over the reservations. Ninety percent of Native Canadian families live below the poverty level.

Ward gives the example of the Wikwemikong Indian Reservation in Northern Ontario which the Native Canadians had farmed since the 1800s. They could not afford modern machinery and were still using horses to pull their equipment, while neighboring white farmers were using tractors. By the 1950s, they were no longer farming, most of the families were on welfare, and alcohol abuse was rampant.

Prior to World War Two, Native Canadian children were sent to religious boarding schools for education. The teachers were second-rate, and they imposed white culture on their Native Canadian pupils. They alienated the children from their own culture, turned them against the white culture, and provided no skills useful for their later lives. In the 1950s, the government took over the education, and its failure is documented by the fact that 94 percent of Native Canadian do not graduate from high school. (Ward noted that Native Canadian parents contribute to this by not exerting more pressure on their children to attend and excel at school—the parents are very permissive with their children and demand little of them.) In the last thirty years, Ward noted that only 525 Native Canadians had achieved a university education. Twenty-four percent of the Native Canadians are illiterate.

Comment

Young (1990) surveyed twelve introductory criminal justice books used in the 1980s and found no mention of crime in Native Americans, although problems of crime in African Americans were included in great detail. Native Americans appear to be the most troubled minority group, with high rates of violence, alcoholism, poverty, incarceration and early death. With a population of over two million, Native Americans are one of the fastest growing ethnic groups and one of the youngest.

However, aside from the importance of studying crime and the criminal justice system as it operates for Native Americans, the topic is of great academic interest. Do the theories and procedures developed for mainstream criminal justice apply to Native Americans? And, if not, what new concepts and theories do we need in order to discuss and explain criminal justice issues for Native Americans? Or more likely, of the theories already proposed, which have most applicability for Native Americans?

Native Americans, therefore, as well as deserving our attention, also provide a test of the adequacy of our theories and intervention strategies. Let me give an example from a somewhat different area.

In the study of suicide and suicide prevention in Native Americans, recently reviewed by Lester (1997), a study was found of suicide among the Shoshoni-Bannock (Levy, 1988). It was found that all of the cases of suicide in this reservation occurred in only eight families. Thus, the provision of education programs in the schools and comprehensive mental health services for the community, while perhaps good ideas in their own right, would do nothing to alleviate the suicide problem of the community. However, to intervene in these eight families runs the risk of further stigmatizing them and increasing their self-destructive deviance. Thus, conventional strategies for preventing suicide were not usefully applicable to this community.

The same may be true for crime in Native Americans. The causes of criminal behavior in Native Americans may differ from the causes of criminal behavior in other ethnic groups, and the useful preventive strategies may correspondingly differ. We plan in this book to explore the extent to which these possibilities may be true.

REFERENCES

Dobyns, H. F. *Their number thinned.* Knoxville, TN: University of Tennessee, 1983.

Frideres, J. S., & Robertson, B. Aboriginals and the criminal justice system. *International Journal of Contemporary Sociology*, 1994, *31*, 101-127.

Gundlach, J. H., Reid, P. N., & Roberts, A. E. Migration, labor mobility, and relocation assistance. *Social Service Review*, 1977, *51*, 464-473.

Kirmayer, L. Suicide among Canadian aboriginal peoples. *Transcultural Psychiatric Research Review*, 1994, *31*, 3-58.

Kroeber, A. L. Cultural and native areas of native North America. *University of California Publications in American Archaeology and Ethnology*, 1939, *38*, 1-242.

Lester, D. *Suicide in American Indians.* Commack, NY: Nova Science, 1997.

Levy, J. E. The effects of labeling on health behavior and treatment programs among North American Indians. *American Indian & Alaska Native Mental Health Research*, 1988, *1*, monograph 1, 211-231.

Mikel, D. Native society in crisis. *Crime & Justice* (Ottawa), 1980, *7/8*(1), 32-41.

Sandefur, G. D. American Indian reservations: The first underclass areas? *Focus*, 1989, *12*(1), 37-41.

Satchell, M. The worst federal agency. *U.S. News & World Report*, 1994, *117*(21), 61-64.

Simmons, J. L. One little, two little, three little Indians. *Human Organization*, 1977, *36*, 76-79.

Snipp, C. M. Sociological perspectives on American Indians. *Annual Review of Sociology*, 1992, *18*, 351-371.

Thornton, R. *American Indian holocaust and survival.* Norman, OK: University of Oklahoma, 1987.

Ward, J.A., Fox, J., & Evans, A.L. Suicide and the Canadian Indians. In V. Aalberg (Ed.) *Proceedings of the 9th International Congress of the International Association for Suicide Prevention*, pp. 389-401. Helsinki: Finish Association for Mental Health, 1978.

Young, T. J. Native American crime and criminal justice require criminologists' attention. *Journal of Criminal Justice Education*, 1990, *1*, 111-116.

Chapter 2

THE PERSONAL AND SOCIAL CONDITIONS
OF NATIVE AMERICANS

Native Americans have high rates of many personal and social problems which may impact upon the occurrence and frequency of their criminal behavior. In this chapter, we will review some of these problems.

Health Problems

General Health

Mahoney et al. (1989) studied the Seneca nation from 1955 to 1984 and found that the men and women had excess mortality from infectious diseases, diabetes mellitus, cirrhosis of the liver and accidents and injuries. The men also had excess mortality from atherosclerosis and hernia/intestinal obstruction, while the women had excess mortality from pneumonia, chronic nephritis and homicide. Both sexes had a deficit of deaths due to malignant neoplasms and circulatory diseases.

Grossman et al. (1994) surveyed several counties in Washington state in 1981 to 1990 and found that the Native Americans and Alaskan Natives, like the African Americans, had a high incidence of low birth weight babies, premature births, and teenage and single mothers, were more likely to smoke during pregnancy and less likely to receive prenatal care than whites. The Native Americans were more likely to consume alcohol during pregnancy than other ethnic groups.

Infant mortality in Native Americans and African Americans was higher, as was general mortality for all ages up to 64. Native American mortality was especially high for pneumonia and influenza, liver disease, and unintentional injury, but lower from cancer than for African Americans and whites. The Native Americans also had the highest rates of hepatitis A and B and tuberculosis, and their rates of chlamydia, syphilis and gonorrhea were higher than those for whites but lower than those for African Americans.

Among the Native Americans, urban and rural groups differed. Rural Native Americans were less likely to have low birth weight babies and more likely to die from heart disease, unintentional injury and cerebrovascular disease, and from firearms.

Sullivan (1989) found that Native American babies in Arizona in 1984 to 1986 had slightly lower mortality rates in the first month and slightly higher mortality rates in the first year than white babies, but much lower mortality rates in both periods than African American babies.[1] Both Native American and African American mothers received less prenatal care than the white mothers. Olson, et al. (1990) found that Native American children (aged 0 to 14) experienced the highest mortality from all external causes combined in New Mexico from 1958 to 1982 as compared to Hispanic and non-Hispanic white children.

However, a survey of Native Americans and whites in the same region (Sugarman et al. 1992) revealed few differences in behavioral risk factors such as seat belt use, drinking, high blood pressure, sedentary life-style, and smoking, although a greater proportion of Native Americans were overweight.

In Alberta (Canada) in 1976, Native Canadians were more likely than whites to die from accidents, suicide and homicide and less likely to die from physical diseases such as heart disease and cancer (Jarvis and Boldt, 1982). Native Canadian deaths occurred at a younger age and more often in non-hospital settings. Trovato (1988) found that, although the mortality rate for Native Canadians in Canada as a whole declined from 1951 to 1971, their mortality rate still exceeded the rates for English-speaking and French-speaking Canadians. Similar results have been found for Native Canadians in the Northwest Territories (Young et al., 1992)–while mortality from "other accidents" has decreased, mortality from suicide, homicide and motor vehicle accidents increased from 1961 to 1980.

---

1. Mortality rates for Native American babies had declined from 1876 to 1986.

The higher mortality rate among Native Americans, combined with the small communities and extended family networks, results in an endless stream of funerals and grieving for the communities (Horejsi et al., 1992).

Substance Use and Abuse

Drug and alcohol use is common among Native Americans. For example, in a survey of Native American students at a post-high school institution, 95 percent had tried beer, 70 percent marijuana, 36 percent amphetamines, 31 percent inhalants, 22 percent barbiturates, 21 percent hallucinogens, 13 percent cocaine, and 6 percent heroin (Goldstein et al., 1979). Some studies find the use of some drugs (such as marijuana) to be more common among Native American youth than among white youth while the use of other drugs (such as hallucinogens and cocaine) are less common (Cockerham et al., 1976). Strimbu et al. (1973) studied students at a southeastern state university and found that Native Americans ranked first out of five ethnic groups in the use of tobacco, marijuana, glue, narcotics, stimulants, hallucinogens, LSD and depressants, and second in alcohol. Inhalant use is particularly common among Native American youths, probably because inhalants are easy to obtain, inexpensive, and produce a high rapidly (Young, 1987).

On the other hand, Holmgren et al. (1983) found no differences in the quantity or frequency of drinking between Shoshone/Arapahoe and white high school students in a rural community. The two groups did not differ either in alcohol-related complications, such as motor vehicle accidents or disrupted friendships, although the Native American students did score higher on a measure of alienation.

Young (1988), in a recent review of research on substance use and abuse, noted that the incidence of substance abuse varies greatly between tribes and is affected by the socioeconomic status and degree of acculturation of the tribes. With regard to alcohol use, Young noted that the majority of published reports indicate a heavier use of alcohol among Native Americans than whites, but he agreed with May (1982) that a broader survey of all Native Americans might reveal similar rates of alcohol use and misuse in both ethnic groups.

Young concluded that the incidence of marijuana use was probably higher among Native American youth, but there was no good evidence for a higher incidence of usage among Native American adults than among whites. The voluntary use of inhalants among Native American youth was twice that for white youth, and inhalants were typically used by Native American youths before they tried alcohol. Inhalants are easy to obtain and, in rural areas, are often the only available intoxicants. They are cost-effective, the effects obtained quickly, and their use supported by peers. Young could find no reliable evidence for significantly great use by Native Americans of other drugs, including hallucinogens, amphetamines, cocaine and heroin.

We might add that although many studies purportedly report high rates of alcohol and drug use by Native American youth and adults, the majority of the studies do not include a comparable group of whites for comparison matched for social class, region of the country, etc. For example, Olsen and Baffi (1982) studied only a sample of native American high school youth. Forslund (1979) did compare Native American and white school children in Wyoming and found comparable rates of alcohol use in both ethnic groups, although the behavioral consequences (such as passing out) were more frequent for the Native Americans.

Drug and alcohol use increases the risk of premature death. In the mid-1950s, the crude mortality rates from cirrhosis of the liver were 12.8 per 100,000 per year in whites and 26.7 in Native Americans (Kunitz et al., 1971). The mortality rate varied from tribe to tribe: 6.8 in the Navajo, 20.0 in the White Mountain Apache and 43.2 in the Hopi. Trott et al. (1981) found higher rates of drug-related mortality (93% of which involved alcohol) among Native Canadians than whites in Manitoba in 1976.

Alcohol abuse has consequences that increase the risk of criminality. For example, Delk et al. (1974) noted that a history of arrests for alcohol intoxication was associated with truancy and dropping-out of school among Papago youth. The role of alcohol in Native American criminal behavior will be explored in much greater detail in later chapters.

Fetal Alcohol Syndrome

The high incidence of alcohol abuse in Native Americans results in many infants being born with the fetal alcohol syndrome (McLaughlin et al., 1995). The problem is worse is some tribes than in others. May et al. (1983) documented high rates of fetal alcohol syndrome in the Apache and Ute in the southwest of the United States (five times higher) as compared to the Navajo and Pueblo. The fetal alcohol syndrome increases the risk of conduct problems in adolescence, including cheating, lying, stealing, and poor socialization. Depression, poor intelligence and attention deficit disorder are also common consequences.

Obesity

Harrison and Ritenbaugh (1992) noted a high prevalence of obesity among Native Americans, along with a high incidence of non-insulin-dependent diabetes, especially in some tribes (such as the Pima). However, Harrison and Ritenbaugh noted that no single major difference in metabolic processes had been identified which could account for these differences.

Social Problems

Poverty

The poverty of Native Americans is great, as we noted in Chapter 1. Some reservations qualify as the "underclass," that is, more than 40 percent of the households have incomes below the poverty level (Sandefur, 1989). Eighteen of the 36 largest reservations met this criterion in 1980. However, in general in the United States, the percentage of poor in 1990 was comparable for Native Americans, African Americans and Hispanic Americans (31%, 32% and 28%, respectively) as compared to 11 percent for whites (Danziger et al., 1994).

Let us look at a description of one reservation. The Standing Rock Sioux Reservation occupies 2.3 million acres in North and South Dakota. Some 6,00 Native Americans and a few thousand whites live there.

> Villages such as Wakpala resemble nothing so much as ghettos grafted onto the lovely, fawn-colored prairie. Near Wakpala, a dump fire smolders, and garbage blows across the buffalo grass. Junked cars sit on dirt front yards, tumbleweed bounces down the streets, stray dogs skulk among the federally built houses. The structures, strewn along the hillside above Oak Creek, are scarred and

mud-splattered. Inside, tiles peel off floors, pipes leak, and the winter wind shakes the dwellings to the core. Villagers generally drive aging clunkers, and the rumble of their engines fills the air. Alcoholics wander the landscape like ghosts. The village's largest structure, a gymnasium built with federal dollars in the 1960s, is riddled with gaping holes and surrounded by rubble. (Montaigne, 1989, p. 25.)

However, not all is bad in the lives of Native Americans and not all Native Americans are in such dire straits. In 1980, for example, Sandefur and Sakamoto (1988) found that Native American and white households were equally often headed by a married couple, with a frequency that was greater than for African Americans. Furthermore, the average household income was slightly higher for Native Americans, than for African Americans, though both of these family incomes were much lower than those for white families.

There are, of course, differences in the economic status of Native Americans living on reservations and those living in urban areas. Furthermore, many Native Americans living off the reservation do not always identify themselves as Native Americans, and this may be true of those who have risen in economic status. Those known to public agencies and who, therefore, are identified as Native American, are likely to be the least successful of those leaving the reservation.

In addition, the economic status of Native Americans living on reservations varies greatly from reservation to reservation (Cornell and Kalt, 1990). For example, the percentage of the work force employed in 1989 in some Native American reservations ranged from 7 percent for the Rosebud Sioux to 79 percent for the White Mountain Apache.

Fostering and Adoption

For many years, many Native American children were placed with white foster parents or adopted by white families. After the passage of the Indian Child Welfare Act in 1978, MacEachron et al. (1996) documented that, in almost all states, the state adoption rate for Native American children declined. The 1975 rate was 2.98 per 1,000 Native American children; the 1986 rate was 0.23. Indeed, by 1986, the adoption rate was similar for Native American and all other children in the United States, whereas in 1975 the adoption rate for Native American children was three times greater.

State foster care placements also declined in almost every state—from 32.38 per 1,000 Native American children in 1975 to 17.50 in 1986. The Native American rate was six times higher than the rate for other children in America in 1975; in 1986, the rate was only three times higher.

Finally, the foster placement of Native American children in Native American homes increased after the passage of the act. Thus, Native American tribes appeared to be gaining much more control over their children after the passage of the act.

Boarding Schools

During this century, it was common to take Native American children from their families and place them in boarding schools where they were forced to "assimilate" into European culture. Although this system was criticized in a 1928 report (Merriam, 1977), in 1974 there were still 34,000 Native American children (including 8,000 under the age of ten) attending such schools (Johnson, 1981).

Attendance at these boarding schools has been associated with high rates, for example, of droppingout of school and psychiatric disorder (Green et al., 1981). However, not all Native Americans disapprove of the schools, and some activists have fought to keep them open (McBeth, 1984).

Relocation

Relocation of Native Americans to urban regions can be a source of stress. However, those helped to relocate (by the Bureau of Indian Affairs) usually end up with higher incomes than those who migrate by themselves who in turn end up with higher incomes than those who do not migrate (Gundlach et al., 1977).

Pathological gambling

The advent of gambling opportunities of Native American reservations (Cozzetto, 1995) has led to some problems for Native Americans. In a study of alcoholics in treatment, Elia and Jacobs (1993) found that 22 percent of the Native Americans were pathological gamblers versus only 7 percent of the whites. Lesieur (1992) has noted that compulsive gamblers are more prone to commit crimes, primarily to obtain money for gambling, crimes such as check forgery, embezzlement and theft.[2]

Comments

The personal and social problems that are found with a high frequency among Native Americans, while not necessarily directly increasing the risk of criminal behavior, provide a set of disadvantageous living conditions for Native Americans. Therefore, any differences in the occurrence and frequency of criminal behavior must be considered in the light of these conditions and, furthermore, comparisons with the criminal behavior of other ethnic groups should match the samples for these background conditions. For example, if a fair proportion of Native Americans in a sample were taken from their parents and given to foster parents of a different ethnic group, the comparison group should at least be matched for the incidence of fostering, even if the samples cannot be matched for fostering with a different ethnic group.

REFERENCES

Cockerham, W. C., Forslund, M. A., & Raboin, R. M. Drug use among white and American Indian high school youth. *International Journal of the Addictions*, 1976, *11*, 209-220.

Cornell, S., & Kalt, J. P. Pathways from poverty. *American Indian Culture & Research Journal*, 1990, *14*, 89-125.

Cozzetto, D. A. The economic and social implications of Indian gambling. *American Indian Culture & Research Journal*, 1995, *19*(1), 119-131.

Danziger, S. H., Sandefur, G. D., & Weinberg, D. H. *Confronting poverty*. Cambridge, MA: Harvard University Press, 1994.

Delk, J. L., Urbancik, G., Williams, C., Berg, G., & Kahn, M. W. Drop-outs from an American Indian reservation school. *Journal of Community Psychology*, 1974, *2*, 15-16.

Elia, C., & Jacobs, D. F. The incidence of pathological gambling among Native Americans treated for alcohol dependency. *International Journal of the Addictions*, 1993, *28*, 659-666.

---

2. Lesieur, however, did not study Native Americans in this respect.

Forslund, M. A. Drinking problems of Native American and white youth. *Journal of Drug Education*, 1979, *9*(1), 21-27.

Goldstein, G. S., Oetting, E. R., Edwards, R., & Garcia-Mason, V. Drug use among Native American young adults. *International Journal of the Addictions*, 1979, *14*, 855-860.

Green, B. E., Sack, W. H., & Pambrum, A. A review of child psychiatric epidemiology with special reference to American Indian and Alaska Native children. *White Cloud Journal*, 1981, *2*(2), 22-36.

Grossman, D. C., Krieger, J. W., Sugarman, J. R., & Forquera, R. A. Health status of urban American Indians and Alaska Natives. *Journal of the American Medical Association*, 1994, *271*, 845-850.

Gundlach, J. H., Reid, P. N., & Roberts, A. E. Migration, labor mobility, and relocation assistance. *Social Service Review*, 1977, *51*, 464-473.

Harrison, G. G., & Ritenbaugh, C. K. Obesity among North American Indians. In P. Bjorntorp & B. N. Brodoff (Eds.), *Obesity*, pp. 610-618. Philadelphia: Lippincott, 1992.

Holmgren, C., Fitzgerald, B. J., & Carman, R. S. Alienation and alcohol use. *Journal of Social Psychology*, 1983, *120*, 139-140.

Horejsi, C., Craig, B. H. R., & Pablo, J. Reactions by Native American parents to Child Protection Agencies. *Child Welfare*, 1992, *71*, 329-342.

Jarvis, G. K., & Boldt, M. Death styles among Canada's Indians. *Social Science & Medicine*, 1982, *16*, 1345-1352.

Johnson, B. B. The Indian Child Welfare Act of 1978. *Child Welfare*, 1981, *60*, 435-446.

Kunitz, S. J., Levy, J. F., Odoroff, C. L., & Bollinger, J. The epidemiology of cirrhosis in two southwestern Indian tribes. *Quarterly Journal of Studies on Alcohol*, 1971, *32*, 706-720.

Lesieur, H. R. Compulsive gambling. *Society*, 1992, *29*(4), 43-50.

MacEachron, A. E., Gustavsson, N. S., Cross, S., & Lewis, A. The effectiveness of the Indian Child Welfare Act of 1978. *Social Service Review*, 1996, *70*, 451-463.

Mahoney, M. C., Michalek, A. M., Cummings, M., Nasca, P. C., & Emrich, L. J. Mortality in a northeastern Native American cohort, 1955-1984. *American Journal of Epidemiology*, 1989, *129*, 816-826.

May, P. A. Substance abuse and American Indians. *International Journal of the Addictions*, 1982, *17*, 1185-1209.

May, P. A., Hymbaugh, K. J., Aase, J. M., & Samet, J. M. Epidemiology of fetal alcohol syndrome among American Indians of the southwest. *Social Biology*, 1983, *30*, 374-387.

McBeth, S. J. The primer and the hoe. *Natural History*, 1984, *93*(8), 4-12.

McLaughlin, T. F., Williams, B. F., Howard, V. F., & Reyes, R. Data-based and effective classroom procedures to assist Native American children with fetal alcohol syndrome and fetal alcohol effects. *Corrective & Social Psychiatry*, 1995, *41*(3), 42-51.

Merriam, L. The effects of boarding schools on Indian family life: 1928. In S. Unger (Ed.), *The destruction of American Indian families*, pp. 14-17. New York: Association on American Indian Affairs, 1977.

Montaigne, F. A shared disgrace. *The Philadelphia Inquirer Magazine*, 1989, February 26, 22-30, 35, 43.

Olsen, L. K., & Baffi, C. R. A descriptive analysis of drug and alcohol use among selected Native American high school students. *Journal of Drug Education*, 1982, *12*(2), 97-102.

Olson, L. M., Becker, T. M., Wiggins, C. L., Key, C. R., & Samet, J. M. Injury mortality in American Indian, Hispanic and non-Hispanic white children in New Mexico, 1958-1982. *Social Science & Medicine*, 1990, *30*, 479-486.

Sandefur, G. D. American Indian reservations. *Focus*, 1989, *12*(1), 37-41.

Sandefur, G. D., & Sakamoto, A. American Indian household structure and income. *Demography*, 1988, *25*, 71-80.

Strimbu, J. L., Schoenfeldt, L. F., & Sims, O. S. Drug usage in college students as a function of racial classification and minority group status. *Research in Higher Education*, 1973, *1*, 263-272.

Sugarman, J. R., Warren, C. W., Oge, L., & Helgerson, S. D. Using the Behavioral Risk Factor Surveillance System to monitor Year 2000 objectives among American Indians. *Public Health Reports*, 1992, *107*, 449-456.

Sullivan, D. A. Conventional wisdom challenged. *Research in the Sociology of Health Care*, 1989, *8*, 197-204.

Trott, L., Barnes, G., & Dumoff, R. Ethnicity and other demographic characteristics as predictors of sudden drug-related deaths. *Journal of Studies on Alcohol*, 1981, *42*, 564-578.

Trovato, F. Mortality differentials in Canada, 1951-1971. *Culture, Medicine & Psychiatry*, 1988, *12*, 459-477.

Young, T. J. Inhalant use among American Indian youth. *Child Psychiatry & Human Development*, 1987, *18*, 36-46.

Young, T. J. Substance use and abuse among Native Americans. *Clinical Psychology Review*, 1988, *8*, 125-138.

Young, T. K., Moffatt, E. K., & O'Neill, J. D. An epidemiological perspective of injuries in the Northwest Territories. *Arctic Medical Research*, 1992, *51*, Supplement 7, 27-36.

Chapter 3

THE FREQUENCY OF NATIVE AMERICAN CRIME

The disproportionate representation of Native Americans in arrest statistics and in prison populations has frequently been noted, both in the past (von Hentig, 1945) and more recently (Krisberg et al., 1987), as well as a differential pattern of crimes, with Native Americans being charged more with alcohol-related offenses (von Hentig, 1945).

For example, Farber et al. (1957) noted a high arrest rate for alcohol-related offenses among the Native Americans in South Dakota. McCone (1966) noted that Native Americans in South and North Dakota had higher arrests rates for crimes against persons but lower arrest rates for crimes against property in 1954 to 1955 as compared to urban whites in South and North Dakota and rural residents in the United States in general. The most common state offense was for public intoxication (77%), and the most common tribal offense was for disorderly conduct and drunkenness (58%).

Jessor et al. (1968) noted a higher rate of court convictions in the prior ten years in Native Americans living in a Colorado town than in Spanish-speaking residents or whites. Schwartz et al. (1988) observed that in Minnesota in 1986, a higher percentage of Native Americans than whites were charged with violent crimes and public order offenses while a lower percentage were charged with status offenses. The same percentages were charged with property offenses and parole/probation violations.

We will review the data on the frequency of Native American crime in this chapter and subject the apparent conclusions drawn by researchers to severe criticism. We will argue that the data as they stand by no means indicate a high crime rate among Native Americans and, furthermore, that the data "as they stand" are woefully inadequate to test whether Native American crime rates are high, average or low because of the failure to control for extraneous variables.

Arrest Rates

Stewart (1964) calculated arrest rates for Native Americans in 1960 from FBI data.[1] Native Americans had an arrest rate of 15,123 per 100,000 per year compared to 5,908 for African Americans, 1,655 for whites, and 1,111 for Chinese and Japanese Americans. The percentage of arrests which were alcohol-related was 76 percent for Native Americans, 33 percent for African Americans, 47 percent for whites and 24 percent for Chinese and Japanese Americans. In fact, "drunkenness" alone accounted for 71 percent of Native American arrests.

Stewart calculated the arrest rates for urban and rural areas of America, and the arrest rates for all four ethnic groups were higher in urban areas than in rural areas, both for alcohol-related arrests and other types of arrests. However, alcohol-related arrest rates were especially high in Native Americans in urban areas. As can be seen in Table 3.1, Native American arrests rates are higher in both urban and rural areas than for the other ethnic groups, but the alcohol-related arrest rate in urban areas for Native Americans is extremely high.

Data from Denver in 1960 from the FBI confirm the same pattern. The arrest rates, calculated by Stewart, were 59,929 for Native Americans, 12,095 for African Americans, 4,785 for whites and 1,136 for Chinese/Japanese/Filipino Americans. The percent of these arrests involving alcohol were 86 percent for Native Americans, 71 percent for whites, 41 percent for Asian Americans and 30 percent for African Americans.

Stewart suggested several possibilities for the high arrest rates for Native Americans, especially alcohol-related: Native Americans are younger, poorer and less educated, they are subjected to discrimination and segregation, they are more likely to repeat offenses and less

---

1. Harring (1982) pointed out that FBI data are incomplete. They are complete for 97 percent or urban areas, but only about 80 percent for rural areas. Most Native Americans live in rural areas. Furthermore, reservation data are not included in the FBI computations. Harring estimated that about half of Native American arrests are missed by the FBI data.

Harring also noted that Census Bureau data are also poor for Native Americans. Many Native Americans live in urban areas for part of the year and on reservations for part. In addition, labeling of ethnicity for off-reservation citizens is often inaccurate.

motivated to avoid imprisonment, and they are further from their residences when committing criminal offenses and so cannot return home as easily when warned by law enforcement officers.

Reasons (1972) reported arrests by ethnic group from FBI data for 1950 to 1968, and his results replicate Stewart's findings (see Table 3.2). Native Americans had higher arrest rates than African Americans and whites, with Japanese and Chinese Americans having the lowest rates. The arrest rates for drinking-related offenses revealed even larger differences. For non-drinking-related offenses, the arrest rate for Native Americans was similar to that for African Americans, both higher than for whites. Looking at the arrest rates in 1968 by crime (see Table 3.2), African Americans had higher arrests rates for all but one crime, with Native Americans second and whites last.

Reasons also noted that Native Americans were over-represented in federal prisons (2.2 percent of prisoners versus less than one percent of the population) and state prisons (1.2 percent of the prisoners).

Jensen et al. (1977) calculated similar data for 1970 from FBI statistics (see Table 3.1) with similar results. Native American arrests rates were higher than those for African Americans and whites for alcohol-related and other offenses and, as was found for African Americans and whites, higher in urban than in rural areas. However, by category type, Native American arrest rates were similar in urban areas to those for African Americans for larceny/burglary/robbery, murder/manslaughter/assault, vandalism, sex offenses, and auto theft.

Looking at possible explanations for these differences, Jensen argued that physical appearance and the resulting discrimination cannot account for the differences between the patterns of criminal behavior between Native Americans and African Americans, even though it may play some role in the high arrest rate for Native Americans in urban areas. (It could not account for a high arrest rate by tribal police, of course.) Since alcohol was prohibited on some Native American reservations, Native Americans from those reservations had to travel to neighboring towns in order to drink, and this would make drunken Native Americans more visible than drunks who resided locally.

Ivy et al. (1981) examined FBI and the Bureau of Indian Affairs data for crime on the reservations for 1975 as compared to crime rates for small towns and rural areas. Reservation homicide, rape and assault rates were higher, but reservation robbery, auto theft, burglary and larceny rates were lower. Reservation alcohol crime rates were higher than those in small towns and rural areas.

Peak and Spencer (1987) analyzed data from the Federal Bureau of Investigation annual crime reports for 1976 to 1985 and concluded that Native Americans were arrested most often for drunkenness (25% of all crimes), followed by driving under the influence (14%), larceny/theft (10%), disorderly conduct (8%), and liquor law violations (7%). Although Native Americans tend to live in rural areas, 75 percent arrests were in cities, 17 percent in rural areas and 7 percent in suburban areas. Over the ten year period, arrests for drunkenness decreased, but arrests for larceny, liquor law violations and drunken driving increased. Arrests of juveniles peaked in 1980, declining thereafter.

On Native American reservations in 1982, 69 percent of arrests involved the use of alcohol or drugs, with public intoxication accounting for about one-third of all arrests.

As we noted in Footnote 1, Harring (1982) observed that FBI data omits Native American crime on the reservations. The Bureau of Indian Affairs does have data on these crimes. In 1976, the FBI reported 104,797 Native American arrests, 81,386 urban and 18,753 rural. The Bureau of Indian Affairs reported 104,022 arrests on reservations.

Harring noted that the crime rates on the reservation were very high. In 1976, the rate of aggravated assaults on reservations was 745 per 100,000 as compared to 128 for the entire rural United States; the murder rate was 21 versus 8 and the rape rate 93 versus 25.

Harring also noted that the tribal variation in crime rates was great. In 1968, the crime rate varied from 5.1 arrest per 1,000 population at Nambe Pueblo to 2,150.8 at the Mescalero Apache reservation. The lowest six Native American arrest rates (all Pueblo) were lower than white arrest rates, while the seven highest rates were on Plains Indian and Apache reservations.

Flowers (1990) reported data from the FBI statistics for 1985 (see Table 3.3). It can be seen that Native Americans had the highest arrest rate for drunkenness and liquor law violations. In general, their arrest rates were higher than those for whites and lower than those for African Americans.

The same trends continued in 1986. Mann (1993) compared the arrest rates for all minority groups in the United States and concluded that Native Americans were disproportionately arrested for victimless crimes. Constituting 0.6 percent of the population, they accounted for 1.0 percent of the total index crimes, 0.7 percent of violent crimes, 1.0

percent of property crimes, and 1.1 percent of non-index crimes. The most common arrest was for drunkenness whereas larceny/theft was the most common crime for African Americans and Asian Americans and driving under the influence for whites and Hispanic Americans. Two-thirds of the arrests of Native Americans were for victimless crimes, the highest proportion of all ethnic groups.[2]

Peak (1994) reported crime rates (per 100,000) for 1992 for the United States as a whole and for Native Americans covered by the Bureau of Indian Affairs (from 200 BIA and tribal police agencies).

Part I Offenses	*USA*	*Native Americans*
murder/manslaughter	9.3	10.6
forcible rape	42.8	32.5
robbery	263.6	162.6
aggravated assault	441.8	273.3
burglary	1168.2	250.5
motor vehicle theft	631.5	67.1

These rates are remarkable in that, contrary to much of the writing on Native American crime, they show that Native Americans commit fewer major crimes than other Americans. Their crimes rates are lower in all categories except murder.

Part II Offenses	*USA*	*Native Americans*
forgery	43.1	15.8
fraud	149.0	48.3
embezzlement	5.7	13.4
stolen property	67.6	72.8
weapons violations	100.7	199.3
prostitution/vice	44.9	3.5
other sex offenses	45.3	228.0
gambling	7.4	2.2
drug abuse	460.5	137.6
disorderly conduct	285.4	2012.7
drunkenness	321.3	4716.9
driving under the influence	621.6	1607.0
vandalism	126.3	868.1

---

2. Mann noted that the crime rates for Native Americans are inflated by numerous and repetitive arrests among a minority of Native Americans.

Here it can be seen quite clearly that alcohol plays a role in the high rates of Native American crime, with Native American rates much higher for the offenses of disorderly conduct, drunkenness, driving under the influence and vandalism. Thus, it is clear that Native Americans do not have high crime rates, but rather high rates of alcohol use and misuse which leads to minor involvement in the criminal justice system. The low serious crime rate of Native Americans is all the more remarkable given their low social status and poor living conditions.

The most recent data available come from the *Sourcebook of Criminal Justice Statistics, 1997* (Maguire and Pastore, 1998), which reports that Native Americans accounted for 1.3 percent of all arrests in 1996, according to FBI data. The only offenses for which Native Americans had a higher involvement than 1.3 percent were liquor law violations (2.4%), drunkenness (2.3%) and vandalism (1.4%). For all other offenses, their involvement was less than 1.3 percent.

Comment

These raw statistics are of some interest, but are inadequate for conclusions to be drawn about Native American crime. Since Native Americans differ so greatly in demographic and socioeconomic characteristics from whites, these differences must be controlled before reliable conclusions can be drawn. For example, since a large proportion of Native Americans live in poverty, the crime rates of these individuals must be compared to the crimes of whites living in poverty— not with the crime rates of all whites.

Silverman (1996) has offered further criticisms. First, he noted that arrest data are different from crime data. Many crimes are not solved (for example, 90 percent of burglaries are unsolved), and so the race of the offender is unknown. Silverman also noted the incompleteness of FBI arrest data, especially in rural areas, and the fact that "race" is missing on forms from some jurisdictions and in others the judgment of race is made by the police officer based solely on his observation of the suspect.

Increasing the problem is the undercount of Native Americans by the Census Bureau because many respondents to the census do not note their race and because prior to 1990 whole tribes did not participate in the census. Silverman argued that only 1990 data are reasonably accurate. Silverman concluded that, for 1990 arrest data, Native Americans did have higher rates of alcohol-related arrests, lower arrests rates for drug-abuse offenses, and slightly higher arrest rates for violent and property crimes than whites, but much lower than for African Americans.

Two findings stand out from this review. If we exclude victimless crimes, then Native American crime rates are not high, even without appropriate controls for factors such as age and social class. Second, reservation crime rates vary widely, and so general conclusions cannot be drawn about all reservations. At the moment, there is little research to suggest causes for the differing crime rates of the many reservations.

Juvenile Delinquency

Armstrong et al. (1996) looked at data from a survey of juvenile crime for 1979 (for those under the age of 18) obtained from the FBI and the Bureau of Indian Affairs. The overall arrest rates were 60.0 per 100,000 for Native American youths, 52.6 for African Americans and 33.9 for whites. Serious crimes accounted for a smaller proportion of arrests for Native American youths than for white or African American youths (10.8% versus 16.3% and 25.8%, respectively), but a greater proportion of less serious crimes and status offenses. For drug and alcohol offenses, the arrest rates were 14.0 for Native American youths, 6.3 for white youths and 2.4 for African American youths.

Women

Lujan (1995) presented data to show that Alaska, Montana and South Dakota had a higher percentage of Native American female prisoners in federal jurisdictions than in the general population of those states, whereas Arizona, New Mexico and Oklahoma did not. Lujan attributed this disparity to racist stereotyping, labelling, paternalism, language and cultural differences, oppression and unresolved grief over the genocide of Native Americans. She presented no data, of course, to test these hypotheses, and she missed an important research opportunity, for the differences in the "excess" proportion of Native American female prisoners between states provides a useful "natural" experiment with which to explore possible causes of the disparity where it exists.

LaPrairie (1989) noted that Native Canadian women in British Columbia comprise about 20 percent of women prisoners but only 5 percent of the provincial population. In Ontario, the percentages were 17 percent versus 2 percent, and in the federal prison 31 percent versus 1.3 percent. LaPrairie noted that the Native Canadian women committed more violent crimes than the non-Native Canadian women, 70 percent versus 32 percent in the federal prison, and 28 percent versus 7.5 percent at the provincial level. The Native Canadian women also defaulted on fines more than non-Native Canadian women.

LaPrairie suggested that the violent crimes committed by Native Canadian women may be in response to the abuse they suffer. Family violence, rape and gang rape, and incest are common in many Native Canadian communities, she argued, and these lead Native Canadian women to respond with violence. However, LaPrairie presented only anecdotes to support her suggestion.

Canada

LaPrairie (1992) cited a number of unpublished reports indicating that Native Canadians have higher crime rates than other Canadians, although the pattern of crimes differs for the two groups. The fact that all of the papers she cites are unpublished makes it impossible, of course, to evaluate their methodology and to see whether they applied any controls for socioeconomic factors.

Hovens (1981) documented that a higher proportion of arrests in Vancouver in 1962 to 1965 involved Native Canadians than would be expected on the basis of their proportion in the population. By type of crime, only for fraud/forgery, indecent assault and murder were Native Canadians underrepresented.

A similar excess of Native Canadians in provincial and federal prisons in Canada has been noted by Mikel (1980). At the federal level, the majority of Native Canadian offenders have committed violent crimes—most commonly robbery and homicide. Compared to non-Native Canadians, Native Canadian federal prisoners have committed assault, theft and homicide more often and drug abuse, fraud and robbery less often. A report in 1977 found that Native Canadian prisoners had more difficulties having their grievances processed in the federal system, were less likely to receive parole or temporary absence passes, and were less often in prerelease centers. Many Native Canadian federal prisoners were ignorant of their rights when arrested or in court, and most felt that their lawyers had not been helpful.

Frideres and Robertson (1994) noted the same excess of Native Canadian prisoners. For example, in 1989 to 1990, 18 percent of provincial prisoners and 11 percent of federal prisoners were Native Canadians (as compared to 5% of the total population). Native Canadian federal prisoners were more likely to have had prior incarcerations than non-Native Canadian prisoners. However, the distribution of sentence lengths appeared to be similar for Native and non-Native Canadians, although the authors did not carry out any statistical tests on their data.

Native Canadians more often plead guilty than non-Natives Canadians and more are found guilty. Fewer Native Canadians opt for fines, partly because they cannot afford to pay the fines. Indeed, many are in prison because of failure to pay fines. Fewer Native Canadians are released on their own recognizance or on bail (which they typically cannot afford).

Incidentally, Frideres and Robertson noted that less than one percent of the police officers were Native Canadians, and the same lack of Native Canadian representatives are apparent throughout the criminal justice system.

Self-Reported Crime

Jensen et al. (1977) surveyed students in a school in Arizona, unfortunately with only a very small percentage of Native American youths (only 1.2%), and found higher rates in Native Americans than in Anglo and Chicano Americans only in fighting, vandalism, drinking and drug use. The groups did not differ in burglary, shoplifting, grand theft, petty theft, assault, smoking, running away, truancy, auto theft, robbery, armed robbery or defying parents.

Robbins and Alexander (1985) surveyed youths aged 10 to 17 in three Seminole Indian reservations in Florida, one urban and two rural. Some 70 percent of the youths completed the self-report scale, about two-thirds were of Hitchitee background and a third of Muskogean background.

Overall, the self-report crime rate was much lower on one of the rural reservations, the most isolated one and the one with its own elementary school. The self-reported rate of vandalism, break-ins and grand theft did not differ in the three reservations. The youths in the urban reservation reported more petty larceny, probably because of the proximity of many stores. Battery (based on interviews with the youths, probably including fist-fights, extortion and gang rape) were also more common in the youths from the urban reservation. Car theft was most common in the rural reservation with more Anglo contact, but Robbins and Alexander felt that the wording of their question on the survey would have included borrowing someone's car without permission just to drive somewhere on the reservation rather than true theft.

Despite the differences in the patterns of offenses on the three reservations, Robbins and Alexander felt that their results confirmed the well-documented urban-rural difference in crime (with higher crime rates in urban areas) in America in general (e.g., Laub, 1983).

Forslund and Cranston (1975) surveyed ninth, tenth, eleventh and twelfth-grade Native American and Anglo students in two high schools in Wyoming with a self-report inventory for 29 types of delinquent behaviors. Considering the proportion of students reporting such behaviors during the past year, the Native American boys differed on seven behaviors: they were more likely to have been truant from school for an entire day, skipped school for some period, taken things from desks/lockers, beaten up someone in a fight and used drugs other than marijuana for pleasure, while the Anglo boys were more likely to have made anonymous telephone calls and drunk alcohol when parents were absent.

The girls differed on 16 behaviors: the Native American girls were more likely to have been truant from school for an entire day, skipped school for some period, signed someone else's name to an excuse, run away from home, let air out of tires, broken windows, broken clotheslines, put paint on objects, taken things from desks/lockers, taken things worth less than $2, things worth $2 to $50, and things worth over $50, driven a car without a license, fought or beaten up someone in a fight and smoked marijuana. Forslund and Cranston also controlled for social class and found similar trends for middle-class, working-class and lower-class boys and girls, although the particular behaviors differed in each comparison.

Forslund and Cranston concluded, although the Native American and Anglo students were similar for many delinquent behaviors, when differences emerged, the majority indicated a greater tendency to delinquency and misbehavior among the Native American students.

Predicting Urban Arrest Rates

Sorkin (1969) looked at the arrest rates of Native Americans who participated in two programs: (1) a direct employment program run by the Bureau of Indian Affairs in which the person and his family are moved to an urban area and assisted in obtaining housing and a job and; (2) a vocational training program in urban areas for Native Americans.[3] In 1963, 1,678 Native Americans participated in the direct employment program and 2,885 in the vocational training program. Samples were selected from each group and followed up in 1966 and 1968, and the earnings of both groups improved after the programs. Those in the direct employment program showed a 58 percent decline in arrests after the program, and those in the vocational training program a 38 percent decrease.

Graves (1970, 1971) studied 259 male Navajo migrants to Denver over a ten year period, who received some assistance for the Bureau of Indian Affairs office there, and calculated arrest rates. The Navajo had arrest rates of 104,000 per 100,000 man-years in the city as compared to 12,500 for Spanish American male migrants and 5,000 for lower-class Anglo males. Ninety-three percent of the Navajo arrests were for drinking-related offenses.

Graves noted that poverty was not an adequate explanation of the ethnic differences in arrest rates since half of the Navajo migrants to Denver never have contact with the police and drink within limits.

The arrest rate for the Navajos was higher in those with:

(1) more unemployment,
(2) lower starting wages,
(3) wages which were lower than before they migrated,
(4) fathers who had traditional occupations,
(5) poorer families on the reservation,

---

3. established as a result of the Indian Vocational Training Act passed in 1956.

(6) less education,

(7) more traditional Navajo values,

(8) weaker commitment to economic/material goals,

(9) more pessimistic future expectations, in Denver or back on the reservation,

(10) high achievement motivation,

(11) some kin and friends already in Denver, and

(12) exclusively Navajo friends in the city, and in those

(13) who were single and stayed single and who were unskilled.

Unfortunately, at the time of this study, multiple regression techniques were not well-known, and so a full multiple regression on these variables was not carried out by Graves. However, his results indicate that many of these variables did interact to cause very high arrest rates.

Graves concluded that the highest rates of arrests were found in those who were least successful in obtaining economic rewards in Denver, who had the worst opportunities for acquiring skills, who experience the greatest discrepancy between the personal goals and their expectations of achieving them, and who have the strongest social pressures to drink and the weakest social controls against drinking.

Williams et al. (1979) surveyed 96 Native Americans in Seattle in 1972 to predict the number of their self-reported arrests in the prior five years. In a multiple regression, the significant predictors were age, mental illness, marital adjustment, marital happiness and awareness of social agencies (negatively), social adjustment, degree of "Indianness" and having a drinking problem (positively) and being male.

Reservation Statistics

Montana

Austin (1984) noted that the crime index for Montana in 1980 was 4437 per 100,000. On the seven Native American reservations, the crime index ranged from 1249 to 3284, with a median of 1470, well below the state average.

Warm Springs Reservation

The Warm Springs Reservation in Oregon (created in 1855 and covering 1,000 square miles of the Columbia Plateau in central Oregon) is the only reservation in that state with tribal sovereignty, and in recent years it has been a prosperous reservation, with income from its forestry industry and from its hot springs resort (Kah-Nee-Tah). Its unemployment rate of 8.2 percent in the mid-1970s was comparable to that for Oregon as a whole (9.1%). The prosperity of the reservation permitted the tribal council to give each adult $60 a month in the 1970s. Children received $45, and $15 was put into savings for them. The population was 2,179, including 1,050 under the age of eighteen (O'Brien, 1977). Despite the good economic and social conditions of the tribe, the rates of alcoholism and delinquency are quite high, suggesting that economic development may intensify social disorganization.

O'Brien (1977) noted that, as with other reservations in the United States, the tribal court was permitted only to imprison people for six months and fine them $500 in the 1970s. All adults committing felonies were handled by the state. Although the tribal laws paralleled Oregon's laws, the tribal laws prohibited more behaviors (such as illicit cohabitation, unnatural sexual acts, and the transmission of sexual diseases) and had harsher penalties for drug use. Possession and consumption of alcohol was prohibited (except at the tourist resort). A decision by the United States District Court (*United States v. Switzler, 1975*) allowed the tribal courts to handle all juvenile cases, regardless of the severity of the crime.

Juvenile complaints are filed by the tribal police and are then referred to a juvenile officer who can dismiss the case, return the youth to the custody of his or her parents, place the youth on probation, or send the youth to court. O'Brien noted that youths on the reservation committing status offenses (curfew violations, truancy, possession of alcohol and illegal use of firearms) are, in fact, more likely to appear in court than youths in general in Oregon (59% in 1972 to 1974 versus 17% for 26 counties in Oregon).

The law enforcement department on the reservation had ten uniformed police officers, three investigators, four jailors, five range-riders, one truant officer and one fish-and-game control officer. The jail had six cells which could hold 40 people and one "drunk tank."

Juveniles were placed in cells in the jails by themselves or in the county detention facility. The tribe had plans in the late 1970s to build their own detention facility for juveniles.

O'Brien noted that, for many reservations, the inadequate facilities and lack of trained personnel for juveniles and the indifference to juveniles often leads the state to intervene and remove delinquent juveniles from the reservation. The Warm Springs Reservation has avoided this problem.

In Oregon as a whole in 1973, 7 percent of all juvenile cases were Native Americans although Native Americans comprised only 0.64 percent of the population. Of 1,306 Native American juvenile cases in Oregon in 1973, one-third (440) appeared in the Warm Springs tribal court. Some 55 percent of the cases in Warm Springs were status offenses, the same percentage as for all Oregon juveniles. Only 2.6 percent of the juvenile cases in 1972 to 1974 were for burglary and 1.6 percent for auto theft (as compared to 7.0 percent and 2.6 percent, respectively, for Oregon as a whole).

O'Brien estimated a delinquency rate of 15 for Warm Springs in 1972 to 1974 compared to a national rate of 2.5, and the Warm Springs rate increased dramatically from 1972 to 1974. While truancy violations declined, drug, alcohol, curfew, vandalism and runaway violations all increased. Two-thirds of the juveniles referred to the court in Warm springs were male, about the same proportion as in Oregon as a whole.

Wind River Reservation

Mills (1989) studied felons convicted in federal court for the Arapaho and Shoshone Native Americans on the Wind River Indian Reservation in Wyoming from 1978 to 1988. (The tribal court handled petty offenses.) During this period, 62 people were convicted of felonies, a rate of 73 per 100,000 per year. Seventy-one percent of the crimes were violent, 82 percent of the felons male, with a mean age of 28 years. One-third of the offenders had prior felony convictions, and 77 percent had prior convictions for alcohol-related offenses.

Seventy percent of the felons were drunk at the time of the offense, 82 percent of the violent felons and 38 percent of the nonviolent felons, and 63 percent admitted that they had problems with alcohol.

However, fifteen of the felons, with clear alcohol abuse problems, denied this.

Forslund and Meyers (1974) studied juvenile delinquency on the Wind River Reservation from 1967 to 1971, during which period there were 703 cases of delinquent behavior among the Shoshone and Arapahoe living there. The delinquency rates per 100 were:

	boys	girls
age 8-13 years	3.7	1.2
age 14-17 years	27.3	16.2

Clearly, the delinquency rate was higher in the boys and the older adolescents. Focusing on a cohort of eighteen-year-olds in 1971, Forslund and Meyers found that 48 percent of the males and 35 percent of females had been arrested at least once.

Jensen et al. (1977) noted that Levy and Kunitz (1974) had rank ordered three Native American tribes for the frequency of drinking-related arrests: Navajo, Apache and Hopi. Jensen then looked at the misbehavior rates of youths from these three tribes in Indian boarding schools in Arizona, California and Nevada. The Navajo students had the highest incident rate for alcohol use and violence, while the Apache students had the highest incident rate for theft and drug use. The Hopi students were the best behaved for all these four categories of incidents. However, the Navajo and Hopi students were similar in indices of family disorganization (such as broken homes) and in being referred to the schools by social agencies. Jensen concluded that tribal background was the major factor in predicting the incident rates.

Comment

It can be seen that the majority of arrests of Native Americans are for victimless crimes, primarily alcohol-related. Examination of non-alcohol-related crimes indicates that Native Americans have arrest rates similar to those for African Americans, with a trend in recent years to be less than those for African Americans.

However, major demographic variables remain uncontrolled for in the data reported in this chapter. It is obvious that Native Americans are poorer and less educated than the average American. Thus, Native American crime rates must be compared with crime rates in other ethnic groups matched for social class (or for variables such education and income which can be used to measure social class).

Second, it is also obvious that Native Americans have a lower mean age than members of other ethnic groups. The proportion of adolescent and young adult Native Americans is much higher than the proportions found in other ethnic groups. Since crime is especially common in adolescents and young adults, comparative crime rates must be calculated by age.

Others variables which ought to be controlled for were mentioned in Chapter 2, such as the experience of foster-care which has been common in some generations of Native Americans.

In conclusion, therefore, what is remarkable is that the crime rate among Native Americans, excluding arrests for drunkenness and related offenses, is so low. Given the poverty, youthful age and other characteristics of Native Americans as a whole in the United States, their behavior is overwhelmingly law-abiding, probably more so than other ethnic groups in America of similar status.

REFERENCES

Armstrong, T. L., Guilfoyle, M. H., & Melton, P. Native American delinquency. In M. O. Nielsen & R. A. Silverman (Eds.), *Native Americans, crime and justice*, pp. 75-88. Boulder, CO: Westview, 1996.

Austin, W. T. Crow Indian justice. *Deviant Behavior*, 1984, *5*, 31-46.

Farber, W. O., Odeen, P. A., & Tschetter, R. A. *Indians, law enforcement and local government*. Brookings, SD: State University of South Dakota, 1957.

Flowers, R. B. *Minorities and criminality*. Westport, CT: Greenwood, 1990.

Forslund, M. A., & Cranston, V. A. A self-report comparison of Indian and Anglo delinquency in Wyoming. *Criminology*, 1975, *13*, 193-198.

Forslund, M. A., & Meyers, R. E. Delinquency among Wind River Indian reservation youth. *Criminology*, 1974, *12*, 97-106.

Frideres, J. S., & Robertson, B. Aboriginals and the criminal justice system. *International Journal of Contemporary Sociology*, 1994, *31*, 101-127.

Graves, T. D. The personal adjustment of Navajo Indian migrants to Denver, Colorado. *American Anthropologist*, 1970, *72*, 35-54.

Graves, T. D. Drinking and drunkenness among urban Indians. In J. O. Waddell & O. M. Watson (Eds.), *The American Indian in urban society*, pp. 274-311. Boston: Little Brown, 1971.

Harring, S. Native American crime in the United States. In L. A. French (Ed.), *Indians and criminal justice*, pp. 93-108. Totowa, NJ: Allanheld, Osmun, 1982.

Hovens, P. Between deviance and integration. In P. Hovens (Ed.) *North American Indian Studies* pp. 255-279. Gottingen, West Germany: Edition Herodot, 1981.

Ivy, S. C., Molesworth, C., Stuler, H., & Hunter, D. K. *Crime in Indian country.* Menlo Park, CA: SRI International, 1981.

Jensen, G. F., Stauss, J. H., & Harris, V. W. Crime, delinquency, and the American Indian. *Human Organization,* 1977, *36,* 252-257.

Jessor, R. Graves, T. D., Hanson, R. C., & Jessor, S. L. *Society, personality and deviant behavior.* New York: Holt, Rinehart & Winston, 1968.

Krisberg, B., Schwartz, I., Fishman, G., Eiskovits, Z., Guttman, E., & Joe, K. The incarceration of minority youth. *Crime & Delinquency,* 1987, *33,* 173-205.

LaPrairie, C. P. Some issues in aboriginal justice research. *Women & Criminal Justice,* 1989, *7*(1), 81-91.

LaPrairie, C. P. Aboriginal crime and justice. *Canadian Journal of Criminology,* 1992, *34,* 281-298.

Laub, J. Urbanism, race and crime. *Journal of Research in Crime & Delinquency,* 1983, *20,* 183-198.

Lujan, C. C. Women warriors. *Women & Criminal Justice,* 1995, *7*(1), 9-33.

Maguire, K., & Pastore, A. L. *Sourcebook of Criminal Justice Statistics,* 1997. Washington, DC: Bureau of Justice Statistics, 1998.

Mann, C. R. *Unequal justice.* Indianapolis, IN: University of Indiana, 1993.

McCone, C. R. Cultural factors in crime among Dakota Indians. *Plains Anthropologist,* 1966, *11,* 144-151.

Mikel, D. Native society in crisis. *Crime & Justice* (Ottawa), 1980, *7/8*(1), 32-41.

Mills, D. K. Alcohol and crime on the reservation. *Federal Probation,* 1989, *53*(4). 12-15.

O'Brien, M. J. Indian juveniles in the state and tribal courts of Oregon. *American Indian Law Review,* 1977, *5,* 343-367.

Peak, K. Policing and crime in Indian country. *Journal of Contemporary Criminal Justice,* 1994, *10,* 79-94.

Peak, K., & Spencer, J. Crime in Indian country. *Journal of Criminal Justice,* 1987, *15,* 485-494.

Reasons, C. Crime and the American Indian. In H. M. Bahr, B. A. Chadwick & R. C. Day (Eds.), *Native Americans today,* pp. 319-326. New York: Harper & Row, 1972.

Robbins, S. P., & Alexander, R. Indian delinquency on urban and rural reservations. *Free Inquiry in Creative Sociology,* 1985, *13,* 179-182.

Schwartz, I. M., Harris, L., & Levi, L. The jailing of juveniles in Minnesota. *Crime & Delinquency,* 1988, *34,* 133-149.

Silverman, R. A. Patterns of Native American crime. In M. O. Nielsen & R. A. Silverman (Eds.), *Native Americans, crime and justice,* pp. 58-74. Boulder, CO: Westview, 1996.

Sorkin, A. L. Some aspects of American Indian migration. *Social Forces,* 1969, *48,* 243-250.

Stewart, O. Questions regarding American Indian criminality. *Human Organization,* 1964, *23,* 61-66.

Von Hentig, H. The delinquency of the American Indian. *Journal of Criminal Law &*
    Criminology, 1945, *36*, 75-84.
Williams, L. E., Chadwick, B. A., & Bahr, H. M. Antecedents of self-reported arrest
    for Indian Americans in Seattle. *Phylon*, 1979, *40*, 243-252.

Chapter 4

ALCOHOL AND CRIME

As we have seen above, many Native Americans committing other types of crime are intoxicated at the time of the offense and many of the crimes committed by Native Americans are misdemeanors involving alcohol.[1] For example, In 1963, in Gallup (New Mexico), 98 percent of the arrests of Native Americans were for drunkenness (Ferguson, 1970). Thus, alcohol plays a major role in Native American criminal behavior.

The strength of this connection varied by tribe. For example, Stratton et al. (1978) studied Native Americans in Oklahoma in 1975 and found that the rate of arrest for public drunkenness ranged from 781 per 1,000 for the Cheyenne-Arapaho to 95 for the Cherokee. Stratton felt that the rate of arrest varied with unemployment, but he did not test this association statistically.

Individual cases bring home the pervasiveness of the problems. For example, George Bald Eagle, a resident on the Standing Rock Sioux Reservation in South and North Dakota, was sentenced to six years in prison for negligence in the deaths of his five children, all less than four years of age (Montaigne, 1989). He had drank so much that night that his wife stormed out of the house. He had tried to keep the wood stove alight and had gone to his sister-in-law's house where he passed out. Ashes from the stove started a fire, and smoke from the fire killed the children.

---

1. Honigmann and Honigmann (1945) studied a small town on the Alaska Highway and found that Native Americans did not seem to differ from whites in becoming hostile or agressive when intoxicated.

Alcohol Abuse in Native American Children

Alcohol and drug abuse begins early in some Native American children. Swanson, et al. (1971) studied Native Americans on a reservation in the northwestern United States. They identified 42 children who drank regularly and were intoxicated at least four times a year, 20 boys and 22 girls, aged 2 to 16 (averaging 14.5). When drunk, they tended to become uninhibited and somewhat aggressive and violent. One boy was arrested 11 times between the ages of 11 and 16 for committing thefts and starting fires when drunk. Some 69 percent had a delinquency record for crimes other than drunkenness, and 33 percent were school dropouts.

A fourteen-year-old girl had been introduced to alcohol by her parents when she was nine and had drunk regularly since age ten, up to five cans of beer a day, usually at home. At parties, she drank until she passed out. Drinking helped her forget her troubles and enabled her to have a good time. She had passed out at least 25 times in the previous four years. She had a nephritic syndrome and a duodenal ulcer. She and her sisters had stolen a car while drunk, and so she had a delinquent record.

Twenty of the subjects were followed-up into their late teens. Only two had made an adequate adjustment; the other eighteen were alcoholics. Four had been imprisoned, three hospitalized for psychiatric treatment and two had committed suicide.

Oetting et al. (1988) surveyed Native Americans aged 12 to 16 in schools on reservations. They found that those youths who drank alcohol also used other drugs (such as marijuana and inhalants) more often than nonalcohol drinkers. The alcohol drinkers also had higher levels of deviant behavior, such as lying and cheating, precocious sex, vandalism and crime, and they had a greater acceptance of such deviance.

Differential Treatment of Drunks by the Police

Stratton (1973) rode along with police officers in order to explore their relationships with drunk Native Americans. In the town he studied, near the Navajo reservation, handling drunks is the main business of the police department. In the town of 14,000, the police make about 800 arrests each month for alcohol-related offenses, about 90 percent of all arrests. Almost all the of the forty police officers were English-speaking or Spanish-speaking whites.

The "drunk tank" was a jail room fifteen by thirty feet, sometimes containing over thirty drunks. Arrest was arbitrary, but the rough criteria for arrest were causing trouble, collapsed on the street, unable to awaken and offering resistance. Sometimes drunks were told to move on, sometimes they were driven around for a while in the paddy wagon and then released, and sometimes known trouble-makers were arrested before they were totally drunk. The treatment was occasionally brutal, and the drunks were sometimes abused physically and verbally.

The police varied in their attitudes toward the people and the problem. Some saw Native Americans as moral degenerates who needed to be punished, while other police officers were more understanding and humane. Most thought that the jailing of the drunks was necessary —it protected the drunks from becoming victims of crime and gave them a place to dry out safely—but some saw that this was not a solution to the problem. These officers recommended rehabilitation and employment programs for the Native Americans. The officers noted the difference in the way they treated whites and Native Americans. For example, they drove a white doctor who got drunk regularly home whenever he asked.[2]

Hughes and Dodder (1984) studied students at Oklahoma State University and found few differences in the frequency and quantity of drinking between white and Native American students. The whites tended to drink distilled spirits more and to drink a little more frequently. The whites also drunk more in public places while the Native Americans drank more at home. However, the Native American students, both men and women, were arrested more than the whites for drunken driving and for public intoxication. The percentages who had been arrested were as follows:

	men	women
whites	9.1%	0.8%
Native Americans	17.7%	4.2%

Hughes and Dodder felt that these data suggested prejudice by the local police against Native Americans who drank no more than whites and who drank less often in public places than whites.

---

2. The police, however, appeared to be generally prejudiced against Native Americans. For example, one police officer married to a Native American woman was shunned socially by his colleagues.

The Law

Prohibition

Federal law prohibited the sale of alcohol to Native Americans until the law was repealed in 1953, leaving the legality of the sale of alcohol for each tribe to decide. (Whittaker, 1982). By 1975, only 92 out of 293 reservations recognized by the federal government had legalized alcohol in some capacity (May, 1977; Weibel-Orlando, 1990), that is, about 31 percent of the reservations covering about 23 percent of the Native Americans living on reservations. Thus, most Native Americans living on reservations have to leave the reservation in order to have a drink. May and Smith (1988) noted that some commentators (e.g., Back, 1981) have concluded that prohibition had a negative impact in Native American drinking patterns, resulting in rapid and forced drinking, encouraging flamboyant, risky, violent and antisocial behavior.

May (1986) examined mortality rates on Native American reservations in Montana and Wyoming from 1959 to 1974. The dry and wet reservations did not differ in mortality from homicide, alcoholism or motor vehicle accidents, but the wet reservations had a lower suicide rate.

An important question is whether legalization of alcohol on reservations had any benefits. May (1976) carried out some analyses which indicated that legalization resulted in economic benefits from alcohol taxes, lower arrest rates on and off the reservations, and lower alcohol-related death rates. For example, one plains tribe permitted the sale of alcohol on the reservation for two months in 1970 before instituting prohibition once again. May (1975) compared the total arrest rate for the tribal members in those two months as compared to the same period a year earlier and a year later and found that on and off-reservation arrests declined during the two month period of alcohol sales.

Smart (1979) studied five communities in the northern part of Canada before and after the 1976 law which permitted Native communities to set their own laws regarding the sale of alcohol. In Frobisher Bay, the most isolated of the communities, restriction of sales (no stores were allowed to sell alcohol) was followed by a decline in arrests for public drunkenness, assault and impaired driving. However, restriction of sales in Rae-Edzo (no store sales were allowed) and Fort Resolution (alcohol sales were rationed) had little effect on arrests.

Public Drunkenness

Austin (1984) noted that prior to 1953, when it was illegal to sell alcohol to Native Americans, Native Americans who managed to obtain alcohol had to consume it quickly, leading to more rapid intoxication. After 1953, many reservation still banned alcohol. For example, the Crow reservation in Montana banned alcohol and forbad drunkenness (Austin, 1984). Thus, Crow tribal members had to go to off on-reservation towns, such as Hardin (MT), some 12 miles from the reservation town of Crow Agency. Thus, drinking in the privacy of one's own home was difficult for the Crow, and they had to drive in order to have a drink.[3]

Members of the Crow tribe felt that the tribal police were too quick to arrest liquor violators. The tribal police were under the control of the Bureau of Indian Affairs, which was seen by many tribal members as an extension of white control. The multiple arrests for drunkenness on the reservation lead to lengthy "criminal" records for some Crow which placed them in a bad light should they appear in an off-reservation court.

Austin also noted that the Crow value honesty and do not attempt as much as whites to manipulate the criminal justice for their own gain. They tend to plead guilty, rather than hiring lawyers to defend them, plea bargaining or getting off on technicalities.

Public intoxication was decriminalized in Washington in 1972 (Cohen et al., 1981). Randall and Randall (1978) noted that this change was instituted in Spokane in 1975, after which drunks were taken to detoxification centers rather than jail. The total number of arrests in 1974 dropped dramatically in 1975, both for Native Americans (from 3,076 to 440) and for whites (from 12,613 to 4,573).

Criminal Behavior Related to Prohibition

Prohibition itself fosters some degree of crime. Among the Papago, Waddell (1990) noted that several families operated bootleg businesses on the reservation. He reported that in 1974 there were at least 24 bootleggers within the seven miles of the tribal headquarters at Sells. Some fifty Papagos made a good living selling illegal alcohol.

---

3. There was an occasional Greyhound Bus between the towns.

Regulating the Taverns

Riffenburgh (1964) noted that bar owners are not supervised well by the local police. Bar owners establish their premises close to reservations, charge much higher prices than in the major towns, sell alcohol to juveniles and to those who are intoxicated, short-change drunken patrons, and take valuable jewelry in exchange for cheap wine. These business practices would not be tolerated in white communities, but law enforcement officers do little to prevent these abuses of Native Americans.

Rehabilitation

Grobsmith (1989) obtained data on 110 inmates in Nebraska state prisons listed as Native American. Their mean age was 30, but the modal age was 21. They had been arrested first at the age of 14.5 and had an average of 18.6 prior arrests. They averaged 0.5 incarcerations under a year in length, 1.2 incarcerations over a year in length, and had been in county jails an average of 3.9 times. Twenty-eight percent of the inmates had family members with criminal records, primarily fathers and brothers. The most common offense was burglary, followed by theft, robbery and first degree sexual assault. About three-quarters pleaded guilty, usually as a response to a plea bargain arranged by a court-appointed attorney. The offenders were typically told that they had little chance of being acquitted and were advised to accept the plea bargain.

According to the Department of Corrections, 40 percent of the Native Americans had a drug and/or alcohol problem. According to a subset interviewed by Grobsmith, 87 percent had a drug and/or alcohol problem, while the remaining 13 percent used inhalants. Inmates were introduced to substance use by friends, relatives, parents and siblings, in that order of frequency, and the mean age of initial use was 11.6 years. Only 24 percent of the inmates were raised by their parents, and 47 percent of the inmates had been physically abused.[4]

Grobsmith found that the inmates typically began their criminal careers by drinking and then getting involved in minor offenses such

---

4. Theories of alcohol abuse in Native Americans include alcohol abuse as an expression of anxiety, a result of poverty and unemployment, and a consequence of paternalistic government control, permissive child-rearing techniques, and cultural norms. Parental alcohol abuse, as well as abuse and neglect of children by parents, has also been implicated.

as stealing a VCR or bicycle. Later, drunken groups would steal cars, go joyriding and get into fights. They were usually returned to custody of their parents or guardians who sometimes threw them out of the house. Juvenile pranks involving cars escalated, thefts were carried out to obtain money for gas, and the youths dropped out of school. They then moved from spontaneous minor crimes to planned serious crimes, such as armed robberies to support more serious substance abuse. Forty percent admitted to continued use of alcohol (11%), drugs (16%) or both (13%) even while in prison! Younger inmates saw prison as a holiday (they referred to it as a Holiday Inn!), while the older inmates were more motivated to change their lives of substance abuse and crime.

Thus, Grobsmith concludes that rehabilitation of Native American inmates *must* include treatment of drug and alcohol abuse. However, many inmates resist this because they see alcohol use (and abuse) as normal behavior. Friends and relatives forgive drunken behavior, abused wives bail out drunken, abusing husbands, and alcoholic intoxication is seen as a mitigating circumstance even for serious crimes.

Alcoholic Anonymous has proved to be unsuccessful with Native Americans. Native Americans object to admitting personal weakness, public confession, drawing attention to oneself, and the Christian basis. Grobsmith also found that many Native American inmates could not read the written materials provided to them and were reluctant to admit this. However, Ferguson (1970) found that a more traditional treatment program for the alcohol abusers led to a decrease in their arrests for drunkenness. The 115 who chose treatment had 1,196 arrests in the previous 18 months, but only 258 arrests in the next 18 months. Westermeyer and Neider (1985) treated 45 Native American alcoholics at the University of Minnesota hospitals and followed them up ten years later. Those who showed higher cultural affiliation at the beginning of the study had fewer legal problems in the following decade. (However, cultural affiliation scores at the end of the ten-year period did not predict legal problems during the preceding decade.)

The increase in ethnic identification in Native American inmates makes culture-specific approaches to prevent alcohol abuse much more effective. Grobsmith recommended placing Native American inmates together and fostering this ethnic identification, such as permitting them to wear bandanas in the traditional headband style. Treatment programs including the Sweatlodge and Sun Dance are useful, and the Native American Church, with its emphasis on sobriety is an important adjunct.

In Nebraska, the Native American Spiritual and Cultural Awareness Group in the prison system was aided by the Native American Rights Fund of Boulder, Colorado, in obtaining a federal consent decree in 1974 permitting religious practices, including smoking the Sacred Pipe, access to medicine men, Native American Church services (without peyote) and attendance at the Sweatlodge. Inmates can request permission to attend Sweatlodges and ceremonies such as Vision Quest and Sun Dances outside of the prison.

Clearly, such rehabilitation programs should be established for Native American inmates. It is foolish to release substance-abusing felons back into an environment where they will continue their old life-style partly because no effort was made to introduce them to alternative life-styles while incarcerated. Furthermore, Grobsmith stressed the importance of using Native American counselors in the programs (especially ex-offenders) and training Anglo American correctional officers about these program so that they do not harass Native American inmates (by, for example, accusing them of smoking marijuana in their pipes).

Comment

Because alcohol is banned on many reservations, Native Americans who want to drink have to travel to towns off the reservation, away from their homes, and so they are arrested in cars, doorways, parks and alleys. Why are so many drunken Native Americans arrested? Young et al. (1987) suggested that the arrests are a source of money for some departments. Sheriffs receive fees from both the state and the federal government for each Native American suspect.

French (1994) noted that some officials in Gallup, New Mexico, in 1990 proposed what French called a "bizarre" strategy—setting up a zone north of the city with bars, soup kitchens, motels and ground transportation for Native Americans to drink. Perhaps the suggestion may not be bizarre, especially if the businesses were run by Native Americans? Although part of the motivation was to improve Gallup for non-drinking residents, the resulting decriminalization of drunkenness and the care and support given to intoxicated Native American visitors to the zone would have improved their treatment. It may be better to sleep in a motel bed than in a jail cell overnight. An alternative solution is to find ways of permitting drinking, even to intoxication, in settings near home, so that drunks can sleep in their own beds at home.

REFERENCES

Austin, W. T. Crow Indian justice. *Deviant Behavior*, 1984, *5*, 31-46.

Back, W. D. The ineffectiveness of alcohol prohibition on the Navajo Indian reservation. *Arizona State Law Journal*, 1981, *4*, 925-943.

Cohen, F. G., Walker, R. D., & Stanley, S. The role of anthropology in interdisciplinary research in Indian alcoholism and treatment outcome. *Journal of Studies on Alcohol*, 1981, *42*, 836-845.

Ferguson, F. N. A treatment program for Navaho alcoholics. *Quarterly Journal of Studies on Alcohol*, 1970, *31*, 898-919.

French, L. A. *The winds of injustice*. New York: Garland, 1994.

Grobsmith, E. S. The relationship between substance abuse and crime among Native American inmates in the Nebraska Department of Corrections. *Human Organization*, 1989, *48*, 285-298.

Honigmann, J. J., & Honigmann, I. Drinking in an Indian-white community. *Quarterly Journal of Studies on Alcohol*, 1945, *5*, 575-619.

Hughes, S. P., & Dodder, R. A. Alcohol consumption patterns among American Indian and white college students. *Journal of Studies on Alcohol*, 1984, *45*, 433-439.

May, P. A. Arrests, alcohol and alcohol legislation among an American Indian tribe. *Plains Anthropologist*, 1975, *20*, 129-134.

May, P. A. Alcohol legalization and Native Americans. Ph.D. dissertation, University of Montana, 1976.

May, P. A. Alcohol beverage control. *American Indian Law Review*, 1977, *5*, 217-228.

May, P. A. Alcohol and drug misuse prevention programs for American Indians. *Journal of Studies on Alcohol*, 1986, *47*, 187-195.

May, P. A., & Smith, M. B. Some Navajo Indian opinions about alcohol abuse and prohibition. *Journal of Studies in Alcohol*, 1988, *49*, 324-334.

Montaigne, F. A shared disgrace. *The Philadelphia Inquirer Magazine*, 1989, February 26, 22-30, 35, 43.

Oetting, E. R., Beauvais, F., & Edwards, R. Alcohol and Indian youth. *Journal of Drug Issues*, 1988, *18*, 87-101.

Randall, A., & Randall, B. Criminal justice and the American Indian. *Indian Historian*, 1978, *11*(2), 42-48.

Riffenburgh, A. S. Cultural influences and crime among Indian Americans of the southwest. *Federal Probation*, 1964, *28*(3), 38-46.

Smart, R. G. A note on the effects of changes in alcohol control policies in the

Canadian north. *Journal of Studies on Alcohol,* 1979, *40,* 908-913.

Stratton, J. Cops and drunks. *International Journal of the Addictions,* 1973, *8,* 613-621.

Stratton, R., Zeiner, A., & Paredes, A. Tribal affiliation and prevalence of alcohol problems. *Journal of Studies on Alcohol,* 1978, *39,* 1166-1177.

Swanson, D. W., Bratrude, A. P., & Brown, E. M. Alcohol abuse in a population of Indian children. *Diseases of the Nervous System,* 1971, *32,* 835-842.

Waddell, J. O. Playing the paradox. *Contemporary Drug Problems,* 1990, *17,* 271-292.

Weibel-Orlando, J. American Indians and prohibition. *Contemporary Drug Problems,* 1990, *17,* 293-322.

Westermeyer, J., & Neider, J. Cultural affiliation among American Indian alcoholics. *Journal of Operational Psychiatry,* 1985, *16*(2), 17-23.

Whittaker, J. O. Alcohol and the Standing Rock Sioux tribe. *Journal of Studies on Alcohol,* 1982, *43,* 191-200.

Young, T. J., LaPlante, C., & Robbins, W. Indians before the law. *Quarterly Journal of Ideology,* 1987, *11*(4), 59-70.

Part 2

CRIMES AND MISDEMEANORS

Chapter 5

MURDER

Frederick (1973; Ogden et al., 1970) reported homicide rates[1] for Native Americans from 1959 to 1969 (see Table 5.1) and the Indian Health Service reports more recent rates (see Tables 5.2 and 5.3) from which it can be seen that the rates greatly exceed those for the United States as a whole. However, the homicide rate for Native Americans is less than that for nonwhites.

For 1971, Native Americans accounted for 0.4 percent of all crimes of violence in the United States, about their proportion in the population. The figure was slightly higher in rural areas, where they constitute 3.2 percent of the population but commit 4.2 percent of the violent crimes. Frederick suggested that most murder in Native Americans is unpremeditated and occurs when drinking during brawls. Psychopathic murderers or those with long-standing personality disorders are rare.

May (1986) noted that the age-adjusted mortality from homicide was higher in Native Americans in general than for the general American population (18.1 per 100,000 per year in 1980 versus 10.8) and higher in the Navajo during 1975 to 1977 than in Americans in 1976 (21.9 versus 9.5). However, dry versus wet reservations in Montana and Wyoming in 1959 to 1974 did not differ in their homicide rates (26.5 versus 21.8, respectively).

Bachman (1992) examined homicides committed in the United States from 1980 to 1984 using the Supplementary Homicide Reports collected by the Federal Bureau of Investigation. The homicide rates were 4.6 per 100,000 per year for whites, 9.6 for Native Americans and 33.1 for African Americans. Whites had the highest homicide rates in

---

1. Homicide rates are based on mortality statistics which are calculated from victims, not murderers.

the West South Central states and Mountain states, African Americans in the Mountain and Pacific states, and Native Americans in the Pacific and West North Central States. Thus, the epidemiology of homicide among Native Americans differs from that for whites or African Americans.

Looking at the ratio of the suicide to the suicide plus homicide rates, the ratio for whites in 1980 was 0.72, for African Americans 0.15 and for Native Americans 0.54. Thus, while whites were primarily inwardly-aggressive and African Americans outwardly aggressive, Native Americans appear to have similar self and other-directed aggressive tendencies.

Some regions have especially high homicide rates. For example, Levy and Kunitz (1969) found a homicide rate of 60 per 100,000 per year for the White Mountain Apache (Arizona) in 1965 to 1967, compared to 15.9 for all Native Americans and 5.1 for all Americans. This high rate appears to have been present both before and after the establishment of reservation. In the past, many of the murders were seen as justified by the Apache and represent retaliation and feud killings (Goodwin, 1942).

Kraus and Buffler (1977, 1979) noted higher homicide rates for Alaskan natives as compared to Alaskan non-natives (and higher homicide rates for Native Americans versus the United States population in general). Furthermore, the homicide rate for Alaskan natives rose from 1950 to 1974 while the rate for Alaskan non-natives declined. In the 1970s, the homicide rate was highest among the Athabascans, followed by the Aleut, then the Northwest Eskimo and least among the Tlingit and Southwest Eskimo.

Canada

In Alberta in 1976 a greater proportion of the deaths of Native Canadians was from homicide than for the rest of the population (3.5% versus 0.6%) (Jarvis and Boldt, 1982). In Canada in general in 1988, Native Canadians made up 2.8 percent of the population, but 17.6 percent of the homicide victims (Anon, 1990-1991). The rate of homicide for Native Canadians in 1988 was 14.6 per 100,000 per year compared to 1.8 for other Canadians.

Jilek and Roy (1976) noted that Native Canadians had a higher risk for being murdered in British Columbia than whites. In a study of the federal penitentiaries in British Columbia in 1974-1975, they found that 21 percent of the inmates incarcerated for murder were Native Canadians whereas they comprised only 2.4 percent of the population of British Columbia. However, no Native Canadians were sentenced for capital murder, but they were sentenced more often for non-capital murder and manslaughter than were the whites.

In a study of psychiatric patients in a region of British Columbia, Canada, Jilek-Aall et al. (1978) found that threats of violence and violent acts were more common in Russian Doukhobors than in Native American Coast Salish, and least common in the Germanic Mennonites. The Doukhobor patients were more violent toward property whereas the Salish were more violent toward people. The Doukhobors were more often diagnosed with schizophrenia, the Salish with reactive-neurotic depression and the Mennonites with affective psychosis.

Women

Lujan (1995) noted that Native American women in 1986 to 1988 had higher mortality rates from homicide (those under the age of 65), as well as motor vehicle accidents and alcoholism, than the general population. For women under the age of 45, Native Americans also had higher suicide rates. Lujan noted that the majority of homicides are alcohol-related.

Children

Native Americans babies are more likely to be murdered than white babies. In 1987, Rhoades et al. (1992) calculated a homicide rate for Native American infants under the age of one of 12.2 per 100,000 per year (18.8 for boys and 5.6 for girls), as compared to 7.4 for all Americans (7.9 for boys and 6.4 for girls).

In contrast to this finding for the United States as a whole, in New Mexico from 1958 to 1982, Olson et al. (1990) found no consistent differences in the homicide rates for children aged 0 to 14 between Native American, Hispanic and non-Hispanic groups.

Characteristics of Murderers and Their Victims

Levy et al. (1969) found that the incidence of alcohol intoxication at the time of the murder was similar in violent and nonviolent murders for the Navajo in the period 1956-1965, around 73 percent. Some 68 percent of the murderers had prior records, but the incidence of alcohol-related arrests was similar in the murderers and a group of non-murderers. The median age of the victims was 25-29 and offenders 30-34. The majority of the offenders were male and the majority of the victims female. There were no white victims. The most common motive was a domestic problem with a family member, and shooting was the most common method of killing. A quarter of the murderers committed suicide (all men).

Bachman (1992) noted that Native Americans used firearms less often for murder than the other ethnic groups and knives more often. Native Americans were more likely to kill acquaintances and less often strangers, but did not differ in whether the murder accompanied a felony.

Baker (1959) studied thirty-six Native American murderers in a federal prison, all of whom had murdered on a reservation. The majority had been drunk at the time of the murder, and the murder was violent, with multiple blows, stab wounds or bullets fired. The murderous violence often extended to others in the vicinity. In some cases, the violence was sexual, occurring in the context of rape and involving mutilation of the sexual organs. The murderers typically acted withdrawn and unresponsive after the act, and Baker felt that the behavior resembled catatonic excitement followed by catatonic retardation. The majority of the murderers had intelligence test scores in the 90–110 range, but their educational grade level was quite low (4th grade on average). Twenty-four of the victims were closely related to the murderers, including eighteen wives. Baker felt that most of the murderers were quiet passive people, with a schizoid adjustment. They showed deficient goal formation and low levels of achievement. Most were chronic alcoholics. In prison, they caused few problems, mainly because their schizoid personality kept them out of trouble. Few had release plans, and all three who had been released had returned after parole violations, two after committing a further murder.

French and Hornbuckle (1982) noted, too, that the majority of cases of murder and assault among the Cherokee in Appalachia involved alcohol intoxication and were often victim-precipitated.

Jilek and Roy (1976) studied murders by Native Canadians in British Columbia. Compared to the white murderers, the murders by Native Canadians tended to lack purpose and to be alcohol-connected. The Native Canadian murderers were less educated, more often unskilled, and more likely to have a criminal record for alcohol-related offenses. They were less often psychotic, and their murders were less often sexually deviant. In prison, the Native Canadians felt less stigma, perceived fewer benefits from incarceration, and more often rejected psychiatric treatment.

When Native Canadians kill Native Canadians, it is more often a related female, whereas when they kill whites it is more often a male. The more traditional Native Canadian murderers had less of an adolescent delinquent record and were older at the time of their first murder. These more traditional Native Canadian murderers tended to come from broken homes, with the result that they were raised by grandparents who imparted the traditional culture to them.

Homicide in Different Tribes

Kupferer and Humphrey (1975) compared the homicide rates of the Lumbee in North Carolina, a tribe which does not have reservation status, and the Cherokee, a tribe which does reside on a reservation, and found that the Lumbee had the higher homicide rates. Both tribes had higher homicide rates than the non-Native Americans in the same counties. The counties in which the two tribes lived differed in general in many respects. The counties in which the Cherokee lived had an older and better educated general population but higher unemployment rates and lower average income. The two tribes themselves also differed in cultural norms. The Cherokee disapproved of violence and avoided situations that might provoke violence, whereas the Lumbee placed a high value on courage and its demonstration through fighting if necessary.

Humphrey and Kupferer (1982) reported that in 1974 to 1976 the murder rates of the Lumbee and Cherokee respectively were 43.3 per 100,000 per year and 54.4. These homicide rates were much higher than the rates in the surrounding counties (32.3 and 19.7) and higher than the Lumbee and Cherokee suicide rates (10.3 and 31.1).

Among the Lumbee, those aged 35–44 were at greatest risk for being murdered. However, for the Cherokee, whereas all murder victims in 1972-1973 were over the age of 35, in 1974-1976 all of the murder victims were under the age of 35. The suicide patterns are similar, with the Lumbee suicide rates peaking for those aged 35-44, while Cherokee suicide throughout the period was found only in those under the age of 35.

Thus, Cherokee adolescents and young adults seem to show the most signs of social distress (if homicide and suicide are indices of social distress), and this pattern grew more pronounced from 1971 to 1976. Among the Lumbee, it is the middle-aged adults who seem to be at greatest risk of violent death.

Westermeyer and Brantner (1972) examined mortality among Native Americans in Minnesota, where the majority of Native Americans are Chippewa (95%). Accidental and violent deaths were the chief cause of death among the Native Americans from 1965 to 1967, whereas it ranked fourth for the state as a whole. Three percent of the homicides in Minnesota involved Native American victims, as compared to only 1.24 percent of all the other accidental and violent deaths for the state, and the Native American victims of homicide were younger than other victims of homicide, but did not differ in alcohol intoxication. For the reservations in northern Minnesota, the crude homicide rate for 1960-1964 was 7.0 per 100,000 per year versus 1.3 for non-Native Americans.[2]

Sociological Studies Of Native American Homicide Indian Health Service Regions

Young (1992b) calculated homicide rates for all twelve areas of the Indian Health Service for 1979-1981.[3] The average homicide rate (per 100,000 per year) was 21.9, ranging from 10.3 in California to 42.2 in Aberdeen. Young (1990, 1991d, 1992b; Young and French, 1996) found that the homicide rate was positively associated with the household size, the percent below the poverty level[4] and the suicide rate, but not a measure of relative poverty (the dollar difference between the median household income for a region and for the overall Indian Health Service population, divided by the median household income

2. Interestingly, the suicide rate was lower in the Native Americans in this sample.
3. Aberdeen, Alaska, Albuquerque, Bemidji, Billings, California, Nashville, Navajo, Oklahoma City, Phoenix, Portland and Tucson.
4. This association was also found to hold for both male and female homicide rates.

for the general American population). Young (1991c) found that the homicide rate of the regions was positively associated with the availability of hospital beds, and so a high homicide rate could be a result of inadequate medical facilities for saving lives.

Young (1991a, 1991b, 1992a) found that the homicide plus suicide rate was positively associated with the poverty level and the accidental death rate, but not with the prevalence of venereal diseases (gonococcal and syphilitic infections) or mortality from six other causes of death such as heart disease or cirrhosis. The homicide minus suicide rate was associated with mortality from diabetes, but not with the poverty level or the prevalence of venereal diseases.

Lester (1995) reanalyzed these data and found that the homicide rate in these regions was not significantly associated with the number of households, median income, persons per household, percent employed, percent below the poverty level, the percentages of the population under the age of six or over the age of 59. However, the best predictors of the homicide rates in a backward multiple regression were median income and poverty (both with positive regression coefficients).

Young and French (1997) calculated homicide rates for children aged one month to 14 months for these regions and found that the homicide rate for these children was positively associated with the percentage of women in the labor force. The more women worked, the higher the rate with which babies were murdered.

States

Lester (1994) found that white and Native American homicide rates were not associated over the states of America in 1980, for all 48 continental contiguous states, nor for the 25 states with large Native American populations (over 10,000).

Lester (1997) collected a large data set for the 48 continental contiguous states in 1980, including 39 social and economic variables. A factor-analysis revealed eight independent factors which Lester labeled: urban/wealth, age, southern, social disintegration, unemployment, labor force participation, Native American population and population density. Native American homicide rates were higher in states with greater social disintegration, and lower unemployment.[5] This pat-

---

5. The same correlates were found for a reduced sample of 25 states with large Native American populations.

tern was quite different from the correlates of the white homicide rate which was higher in the south, in states with a larger Native American population and where social disintegration was higher.

Lester (1996) examined Native American homicide rates over time from 1955 to 1987 and found that the national unemployment rate was not associated with the Native American homicide rate.

Bachman (1991, 1992) examined the influence of two social factors on Native American homicide rates—social disorganization and economic deprivation. For the 27 states of America with reservations, the homicide rate in 1980-1984 was moderately associated with Native American unemployment rates while divorce rates, the percentage of the Native American population aged 15-24, the percentage living in poverty and the percentage of Native Americans in the state were not associated with the Native American homicide rate.

For 114 counties containing reservations, the Native American homicide rate was associated only weakly with economic and social variables. However, an index of poverty (including poverty, unemployment and high school dropout rates) and social disorganization (female heads of households and recent arrivals to the reservation) were associated with Native American homicide rates in a multiple regression analysis.[6]

Bachman felt that her study indicated that both social disorganization and economic deprivation contribute to the etiology of Native American homicide, but the results of her study were inconsistent (differing at the state and county levels) and rather weak. She considered other theories, including the possibility of discrimination in the criminal justice system so that Native Americans are more likely to be unfairly arrested, tried and convicted, poor medical services on reservation so that more assault victims die, and the great abuse of alcohol among Native Americans which increases the chances of violence of all kinds (such as domestic violence) and, therefore, murder. However, she did not test these theories empirically.

---

6. At the univariate level, only the percentage of high school drop-outs predicted the homicide rate. Although the two indices (of poverty and social disorganization) predicted homicide rates, the percentage of Native Americans in the counties and the percentage of people aged 18-24 did not.

Cultural Patterns or Acculturation Stress?

Levy and Kunitz (1969, 1971, 1974) reported homicide rates for several Native American tribes for the period 1883 to 1889:

Eastern Pueblo Agency	1.9
Navajo	5.9
South Plains	
Kiowa-Comanche	14.2
Southern Cheyenne	13.2
North Plains	
Pine Ridge Sioux	14.7
Yankton Sioux	22.0
Crow	19.0
Fort Peck, Assiniboice	
& Sioux	50.0
Blackfoot	51.3
Basin Plateau	
Fort Hall Shoshone	71.2
Western Shoshone	86.0
Nevada Paiute	130.0
Apache	
Eastern Apache	86.6
Western Apache	165.0

Levy and Kunitz listed these tribes above in order of the degree of social integration. Since the homicide rates increased as one moves down the list, Levy and Kunitz concluded that social pathologies, such as murder, became more common as social integration increased.

Levy and Kunitz felt that modern homicide rates were similar to these: Hopi 6, Navajo 5 and White Mountain Apache 72 per 100,000 per year. Thus, they concluded that social pathologies, such as murder, were a result of long-standing cultural patterns (in particular, the dimension of loosely organized versus tightly integrated tribes) rather than acculturation stress

Levy and Kunitz thought that Native American homicide rates had not increased over the last hundred years (in fact, the Apache homicide rate seemed to have decreased), and neither were they higher during times of stress. The pattern of homicide had not changed either —the dominant pattern among the Navajo, for example, was and is for a married male between 35 and 45 to kill his wife because of sexual jealousy or other domestic problems, often committing suicide shortly afterwards.

Levy and Kunitz thought that alcohol did not play a major role in Navajo homicide. Homicide offenders did not differ in prior alcohol-related arrests (or in arrests for other offenses) from Navajo who did not murder. Furthermore, while the incidence of alcoholic cirrhosis was related to the accessibility of alcohol over the regions of the Navajo reservation, homicide rates were not.

Everett (1975) also tried to argue that social pathology in Native American tribes is a manifestation of traditional patterns of behavior rather than disintegration due to acculturation stress. To do this, he tried to document the incidence of murder and other pathological behaviors (such as suicide) over time in two Western Apache tribes. In the late 1800s, the group at San Carlos were restricted in travel and were forced to become wage laborers. The White Mountain Apache, in contrast, were left alone, free to travel, and exploited traditional economic resources. For example, they sold hay and wood to the military for cash and commissary privileges. Today, however, acculturation is proceeding similarly in both groups.

It proved difficult to get reliable estimates of homicide rates for both groups in historical times. The murder rate for the San Carlos group was 49 in 1873-1905 and 35 in 1962-1968; the corresponding rates for the White Mountain group were 58 and 43. In recent years, the pattern of murder has changed for both groups; there are now more female victims, more female offenders, and more relatives as victims (including spouses).

The problem for Everett was his inability to obtain reliable estimates of prereservation murder rates. He had to conclude, therefore, that his data did not provide support for his thesis. However, the similar patterns for both groups of Apache indicated that the culture clash between Native Americans and whites did not play a large role in determining these patterns. Everett also suggested, again without good evidence since the rates were so low, that murder and suicide varied inversely over time in the Apache and so were functional equivalents.

Comment

It must be borne in mind that some homicides may go misrecorded, especially at the state and federal level. Marshall and Soule (1988) studied deaths occurring in some predominantly Native villages in southwestern Alaska in 1979-1984. The state Vital Statistics recorded 215 accidental deaths for this period. Examination of coroners' files revealed that 24 were determined locally to be suicides and 16 homicides. Everett (1970) noted that, although murder is condemned by the White Mountain Apache, the community sometimes hides the nature of the death from the Anglo authorities. Everett knew of three murders officially proclaimed to be suicides in a twenty year period.

Despite these possible inaccuracies, several conclusions can be drawn from this research on murder. First, traditional patterns of violence appear to have continued and could account for the present patterns of murder in the different tribes of Native Americans.

Second, the rates with which Native Americans are murdered in the different regions are associated with social variables as are the homicide rates of other ethnic groups. However, what is of interest and merits further research is the fact that the correlates of the regional murder rates differ for Native Americans from the correlates identified for other ethnic groups. A sociological theory of these regional rates may be possible, but it will probably differ from the theories proposed for the homicide rates of other ethnic groups.

Clearly, a great deal of research needs to be carried out on Native American murder. Research is needed on reservation versus non-reservation murder and intraracial versus interracial murder among Native Americans, as well as better comparisons between murders by Native Americans and by other ethnic groups.

REFERENCES

Anon. *Statistical profile on Native mental health.* Ottawa: Indian & Northern Health Services, 1990-1991.

Bachman, R. An analysis of American Indian homicide. *Journal of Research in Crime and Delinquency,* 1991, *28,* 456-471.

Bachman, R. *Death and violence on the reservation.* Westport, CT: Auburn House, 1992.

Baker, J. L. Indians, alcohol and homicide. *Journal of Social Therapy,* 1959, *5,* 270-275.

Everett, M. W. Pathology in White Mountain Apache culture. *Western Canadian Journal of Anthropology,* 1970, *2,* 180-203.

Everett, M. W. American Indian social pathology. In T. R. Williams (Ed.), *Psychological anthropological,* pp. 249-285. The Hague: Mouton, 1975.

Frederick, C. J. *Suicide, homicide, and alcoholism among American Indians.* Rockville, MD: NIMH, 1973

French, L. A., & Hornbuckle, J. Indian violence. In L. A. French (Ed.), *Indians and criminal justice*, pp. 131-146. Totowa, NJ: Allanheld, Osmun, 1982.

Goodwin, C. *The social organization of the western Apache*. Chicago: University of Chicago, 1942.

Humphrey, J. A., & Kupferer, H. J. Homicide and suicide among the Cherokee and Lumbee Indians of North Carolina. *International Journal of Social Psychiatry*, 1982, *28*, 121-128.

Jarvis, G. K., & Boldt, M. Death styles among Canada's Indians. *Social Science & Medicine*, 1982, *16*, 1345-1352.

Jilek, W., & Roy, C. Homicide committed by Canadian Indians and non-Indians. *International Journal of Offender Therapy*, 1976, *20*, 201-216.

Jilek-Aall, L., Jilek, W., & Flynn, F. Sex role, culture and psychopathology. *Journal of Psychological Anthropology*, 1978, *1*, 478-488.

Kraus, R., & Buffler, P. Intercultural variation in mortality due to violence. In E. F. Foulks, R. M. Wintrob, J. Westermeyer & A. R. Favazza (Eds.), *Current perspectives in cultural psychiatry*, pp. 81-91. New York: Spectrum, 1977.

Kraus, R., & Buffler, P. Sociocultural stress and the American Natives in Alaska. *Culture, Medicine & Psychiatry*, 1979, *3*, 111-151.

Kupferer, H. J., & Humphrey, J. A. Fatal Indian violence in North Carolina. *Anthropological Quarterly*, 1975, *48*, 236-244.

Lester, D. Native American suicide and homicide rates. *Psychological Reports*, 1994, *74*, 702.

Lester, D. Suicide and homicide among Native Americans. *Psychological Reports*, 1995, *77*, 10.

Lester, D. American Indian suicide and homicide rates and unemployment. *Perceptual & Motor Skills*, 1996, *83*, 1170.

Lester, D. *Suicide in American Indians*. Commack, NY: Nova Science, 1997.

Levy, J. E., & Kunitz, S. J. Notes on some White Mountain Apache social pathologies. *Plateau*, 1969, *42*, 11-19.

Levy, J. E., & Kunitz, S. J. Indian reservations, anomie, and social pathologies. *Southwestern Journal of Anthropology*, 1971, *27*, 97-128.

Levy, J. E., & Kunitz, S. J. *Indian drinking*. New York: Wiley, 1974.

Levy, J. E., Kunitz, S. J., & Everett, M. Navajo criminal homicide. *Southwestern Journal of Anthropology*, 1969, *25*, 124-152.

Lujan, C. A. Women warriors. *Women & Criminal Justice*, 1995, *7*(1), 9-33.

Marshall, D. L., & Soule, S. Accidental deaths and suicides in southwest Alaska. *Alaska Medicine*, 1988, *30*(2), 45-52.

May, P. A. Alcohol and drug misuse prevention programs for American Indians. *Journal of Studies on Alcohol*, 1986, *47*, 187-195.

Ogden, M., Spector, M. I., & Hill, C. A. Suicides and homicides among Indians. *Public Health Reports*, 1970, *85*, 75-80.

Olson, L. M., Becker, T. M., Wiggins, C. L., Key, C. R., & Samet, J. M. Injury mortality in American Indian, Hispanic, and non-Hispanic white children in New Mexico, 1958-1982. *Social Science & Medicine*, 1990, *30*, 479-486.

Rhoades, E. R., Brenneman, G., Lyle, J., & Handler, A. Mortality of American Indian and Alaska Native infants. *Annual Review of Public Health*, 1992, *13*, 269-285.

Westermeyer, J., & Brantner, J. Violent death and alcohol use. *Minnesota Medicine,* 1972, *55,* 749-752.

Young, T. J. Poverty, suicide and homicide among Native Americans. *Psychological Reports,* 1990, *67,* 1153-1154.

Young, T. J. Venereal diseases and aggression management among Native Americans. *Psychological Reports,* 1991a, *69,* 906.

Young, T. J. Poverty and aggression management among Native Americans. *Psychological Reports,* 1991b, *69,* 609-610.

Young, T. J. Medical resources, suicide and homicide among Native Americans. *Corrective & Social Psychiatry,* 1991c, *37*(3), 47-49.

Young, T. J. Suicide and homicide among Native Americans. *Psychological Reports,* 1991d, *68,* 1137-1138.

Young, T. J. Mortality rates and aggression management among Native Americans. *Psychological Reports,* 1992a, *70,* 665-666.

Young, T. J. Household size, suicide and homicide among American Indians. *International Journal of Comparative & Applied Criminal Justice,* 1992b, *16,* 125-127.

Young, T. J., & French, L. A. Suicide and homicide rates among U.S. Indian Health Service areas. *Social Behavior & Personality,* 1996, *24,* 365-366.

Young, T. J., & French, L. A. Homicide rates among Native American children. *Adolescence,* 1997, *32,* 57-59.

Chapter 6

CHILD ABUSE AND NEGLECT

White and Cornely (1981) noted that the study of child abuse and neglect among Native Americans was ignored for many years because of jurisdictional divisions in health, social service and legal programs. The agencies involved had difficulty in coordinating and cooperating. In addition, there was a tendency to attribute some aberrant child-rearing behaviors to cultural differences.

Fischler (1985) noted many other problems. First, some Native Americans view the investigation and prosecution of child abuse and neglect as yet another way in which the dominant white culture oppresses minority cultures. They argue that many of the accusations of child abuse are unjust and result in abuse of Native American children by whites when they remove the children from their families and place them with white families or in institutions such as boarding schools—perhaps as many as 30 percent of all Native American children were treated in this way in the 1960s and 1970s. The Indian Child Welfare Act of 1978 acknowledged this discrimination

The American Association for Indian Affairs noted that the Native American custom of placing children in the extended family was sometimes viewed as abandonment by white officials. Hull (1982) reported the case of John Chasing Hawk, a nine-year-old Sioux who was reported as a possible case of neglect by his teacher when she found out that he had been living for several weeks with a non-related family. Investigation discovered that John's parents were staying with relatives in a nearby town while looking for work, and they had felt that it was in John's interests to remain in his school. John's parents had in fact taken in other children of neighbors in similar circumstances. Similarly, letting siblings take care of children was sometimes viewed as neglect by white social workers. In addition, many Native

Americans live in poverty with no running water or electricity, limited parental education, large families and the use of native healers, and white outsiders may view these conditions as constituting "neglect."

On the other hand, Fischler also noted that the extent of child abuse and neglect among Native Americans may be underestimated. Since prevention and treatment programs for child abuse are rare, mental health officials may be reluctant to report cases. The caseloads of social workers are too large to supervise their charges effectively. Physicians working for the Indian Health Service are typically transients and distrusted by the communities, making it unlikely that residents would report cases of child abuse. The reliance on non-Native health and social service officials may have also contributed to this mistrust.

Reporting child abuse often raises problems for those who report it. Long (1986) gave the example of a neighbor who reported a mother for physically abusing her eight-year-old daughter. The court told the abuser the name of the informant, and the abuser's family then harassed and beat the neighbor. In another case, an uncle raped a seven-year-old girl, whose mother reported the incident to the authorities. Her own family then ostracized both her and her daughter, calling them "sluts."

Fischler thought that this situation might improve after the passage of the Indian Child Welfare Act in 1978 which gave tribal courts jurisdiction over cases of child abuse and provided some funds for programs.

The Indian Child Welfare Act

The Indian Child Welfare Act in 1978 gave jurisdiction to tribal courts over child custody cases proceedings involving children who live on reservations or who are wards of the court. For children living off the reservation, the parents and tribal court must be informed of state court proceedings, and those involved can petition to have the case transferred to a tribal court. The act also laid out rules for state courts and agencies in their handling of cases involving Native American children.

Dietrich (1986) noted that the act led to problems in the coordination of state and tribal agencies and personnel. Sometimes, the Native

American parents live too far from the reservation to return for the tribal court hearing, and some give up custody of their child out of feelings of hopelessness. However, the act does permit the tribe to appoint a representative to attend and participate in state court hearings.

The problem of the placement of Native American children who need to be removed from their parents raises several problems. Although placement in Native American families is preferred, some Native American parents request placement of the children with white families because of the social and economic advantages that they think such placement will provide for their children. Sometimes there are not enough Native American families available for foster care or adoption

Tribal Law

Wichlacz and Wechsler (1983) noted that Native American tribes are not required to conform to state or local laws on any issue, including those pertaining to child abuse and neglect. They identified 79 tribes with written tribal codes on child abuse and neglect, 12 with unwritten codes, and 23 operating under the federal code (*Code of Federal Regulations*, Title 25, Part II, 1981). At the time of writing, Wichlacz and Wechsler noted that many of the tribal codes had not been revised for some fifty years.

There is no comprehensive compilation of tribal legal codes, but Wichlacz and Wechsler analyzed 51 tribal codes on child abuse and neglect. Only 12 codes had specific provisions for child abuse and neglect, although most of the codes (96%) proscribed specific acts against children that are usually defined as child abuse and neglect. However, the definition of child abuse and neglect and the acts prohibited varied widely from tribe to tribe. The reporting and recording of cases is also not addressed universally and uniformly by the codes.

In general, Wichlacz and Wechsler noted, the tribal courts proceed much like state courts, with provisions for the right to be represented, appointment of a person to represent the child's interests, medical and psychiatric evaluations and social studies, and termination of parental rights.

Child Sexual Abuse by Outsiders

French (1994) documented several cases in which non-Native teachers and other professional staff working with Native Americans, often in the employ of the federal government, were active pedophiles and molested large numbers of Native American children. The Bureau of Indian Affairs was one of the major culprits in this, failing to have reporting guidelines for child abuse and failing to have background checks on employees. French reported one case in which the Bureau was warned by previous employers about one teacher, but merely lectured the other staff on the dangers of slander!

Research

Sexual Abuse

Fischer (1983) identified 26 girls and boys (aged 13 to 18) who were victims of sexual abuse seen at a psychiatric institute in Alaska. Forty-six percent were Native Americans or Alaskan Natives, whereas only about 17 percent of the population was Native American or Alaskan Native.

Carter and Parker (1991) studied records at the Division of Indian Work in Minneapolis/St. Paul which serves Native Americans in the Twin Cities and those who visit from the Chippewa (Ojibwa) and Sioux (Dakota) reservations in the state. A survey of files revealed 41 clear cases of incest with 39 female victims and two male victims from January 1986 to August 1988.[1] Most of the victims were women in their early 20s who reported incest from many years before by perpetrators geographically distant or dead. Fathers and persons in parental roles accounted for 44 percent of the incidents, other relatives 34 percent and siblings 22 percent.

Thirty-six cases had more complete data. Of these, 25 victims were assaulted by two or more perpetrators, while eight were assaulted many times by one perpetrator. Parental and sibling violations usually involved single perpetrators, while abuse by other relatives typically involved many perpetrators.

Carter and Parker suggested that the causes of incest for these perpetrators might include experiences at government boarding schools

---

1. Minnesota had a population of about 45,000 Native Americans in 1980.

to which many of the Native Americans who are now parents were sent. Parental modeling in these schools was absent, and some of the children in the schools were sexually abused by the staff. This would be an interesting hypothesis to explore, but no research data has yet compared the behavior of Native American parents who attended the boarding schools and those who did not.

Informants told Carter and Parker that incest did not occur in the precolonial times, and Native Americans today sometimes blame whites for its occurrence. Native Americans value noninterference and so do not report all cases, and victims tended not to report fathers and siblings until many years after the incidents. Native Americans also fear public authorities, especially child protection services who are viewed as depriving mothers of their own children.

Blum et al. (1992) studied over thirteen thousand 7th to 12th graders in schools serving reservation communities. Overall, 13 percent of the youths reported physical abuse and 10 percent sexual abuse. Blum estimated that this prevalence was twice as great as that reported by rural white youths in Minnesota. (Blum gave the prevalence for females as 19 percent and 17 percent respectively, but did not report the prevalences for males.) The prevalence of abuse was higher in Native Alaskans than in Native Americans (26% versus 15%).

Robin et al. (1997) surveyed three reservations in the southwest and found that 49 percent of the women and 14 percent of the men reported childhood sexual abuse (before the age of 15), percentages which Robin felt were comparable to the prevalence for whites in America. The typical abuse was by a member of the extended family, by a single perpetrator, when the child was aged 6 to 9, and involved penetration with a penis or other object. The severity of the abuse seemed to Robin to be comparable to that found in Americans in general.

Males and females who were sexually abused were more likely as adolescents to be expelled from school, break rules, be arrested, appear in juvenile court, lie, steal, break and destroy property, run away from home and have voluntary sex. This pattern continued into adulthood, although there were no differences in felony arrests. Those who were sexually abused were more likely to have a psychiatric diagnosis as adults, including antisocial personality disorder (more commonly known as the psychopath or sociopath), drug abuse and affective disorder (that is, depressive disorders).

The younger subjects were more likely to report childhood sexual abuse, but this may be due to an increase in sexual abuse in recent years, memory loss in the older subjects, or a reluctance in the older subjects to disclose this.

It is striking that some reports make the sexual abuse of Native American children seem commonplace. In a study of Native Americans seen at an HIV clinic in San Francisco (Rowell and Kusterer, 1991), all three cases reported sexual abuse. Jack, a Crow from Montana, was sexually abused by an uncle and a neighbor while Charlene, a Pomo from California, was sexually abused by two of her mother's boyfriends and by several neighbors.[2]

Physical Abuse And Neglect

Nagi (1977) provided estimates the incidence of child abuse and neglect in Florida in 1972 based on official reports. The rates per 1,000 children were:

white male	15.2
white female	16.0
black male	13.3
black female	14.1
oriental male	8.8
oriental female	9.4
Native American male	6.5
Native American female	2.7
Spanish American male	1.1
Spanish American female	1.2
other male	19.6
other female	23.8

It can be seen that the incidence for Native American children was less than that for white, black and oriental children, but higher than that for Spanish-speaking children.

Wichlacz et al. (1978) studied the Cheyenne River Sioux Indian Reservation in South Dakota and found 65 cases of reported child

---

2. In addition, Mark, a Klamath from Oregon was brutally beaten by foster parents.

abuse and neglect from September 1974 through December 1975. The median age of the children was 2 (and the mean was 4.5 years), and fifty-two percent of the children were male. Sixty-five percent of the cases were neglect and 35 percent abuse. The police made the initial contact in 65 percent of the cases. The most common types of abuse and neglect were malnutrition and abandonment. The rate of abuse and neglect for the reservation in 1975 was estimated to be 11 per 1,000 Native American persons per year.

Lujan et al. (1989) studied all of the abused and neglected children in one region in the southwest for a couple of years. They identified 117 children, mostly Pueblo, of whom 64 percent had been both abused and neglected, 22 percent neglected, 4 percent abused and 9 percent neither abused nor neglected. The typical incident involved the biological mother, and both the parents and grandparents were alcohol abusers. About a third of the children were physically or mentally handicapped,[3] and about half of the children were found to be acting out with maladjusted behavior. The parents and grandparents frequently had a history of having been abused themselves as children and came from alcoholic families with a history of violence.

For the children, statistical analysis indicated that abuse was more common in female children who have experienced many moves from home to home, whereas neglect was more common where there was a family history of alcohol abuse. However, the sample of children did not include many without abuse or neglect, and so these results are of limited value in predicting patterns of abuse and neglect in the community.

Piasecki et al. (1989) surveyed 1,155 Native American children and adolescents in thirty-three reservations in the Albuquerque and Phoenix areas in 1984 to 1986.[4] Sixty-seven percent were neglected or abused (37 percent were both neglected and abused, 21 percent neglected, and 9 percent abused). For neglect, emotional neglect was most common followed by physical neglect and medical neglect. For abuse, emotional abuse was most common followed by physical neglect and sexual abuse. More boys than girls were neglected, while more girls than boys were abused. The percentage of children abused increased with age while the percentage neglected decreased with age.

---

3. It was not clear whether these handicaps preceded the abuse and neglect or were a result of the abuse or neglect.

4. 20.5% of the children had chronic medical conditions, 9.5% physical disabilities and 0.4% mental retardation. Eighteen percent received psychiatric diagnoses.

Abuse and neglect was more common in children sent to boarding schools and even more common in those in foster or adoptive homes. Abuse and neglect were more common if the parents abused alcohol or were divorced and if the families were chaotic or single-parent homes. Children both abused and neglected showed the most psychiatric symptoms, but abuse and neglect was not associated with substance use. Abused and neglected children were more likely to run away from school or be expelled.

White and Cornely (1981) obtained data on cases of child abuse and neglect for 1975 from 29 agencies and sources involved with the Navajo Nation located in Arizona, New Mexico and Utah. They located 365 cases of abused or neglected Navajo children under the age of nine and 867 comparison children drawn from medical facilities. Of the 365 abused or neglected children, 264 (72%) lived on the reservation and 101 (28%) in surrounding communities. Two of the children died from the abuse, and 117 (32%) received medical care. Only 55 children had their cases handled by the courts. Fifty two of the children were abused, 220 classified as voluntary neglect and 93 as involuntary neglect. The rate of abuse or neglect for the reservation children was 10.34 per 1,000 children, but there was a large regional variation—from 15.75 in Fort Defiance to 6.72 in the Western region.

The abused and neglected children came from larger families (that is, they had more siblings), their parents were less often married, their mothers and fathers were older, and the income from their families was more likely to come from government sources. The abused or neglected children did not differ in age, sex or ethnicity[5] from the comparison children. They did not differ in the incidence of low birth weight, mental retardation or chronic physical handicaps.

Comparing the abused with the neglected children, White and Cornely found that the abused children less often sustained severe injuries and were more often referred for social services and less often for medical care. They did not differ in ethnicity or the marital status of their parents. The abused and involuntarily neglected children were more likely to stay in their own homes, whereas those experiencing voluntary neglect were less likely to do so.

Oakland and Kane (1973) compared Native American Navajo mothers who had neglected their children with those who had not done so and found no differences in the incidence of working moth-

---

5. Whether one or both parents were Navajo.

ers. The mothers who had neglected their children were less often married (and more often single, divorced or widowed) and had fewer siblings. The two groups did not differ in prenatal care, their age when the baby was born, or in educational level. The neglected children did have lower birth weights.

Oakland and Kane found that most of the working mothers left their children with relatives, and so work per se did not appear to be an important factor in neglect. The most common types of neglect were, in order: poor home situation, malnutrition, failure to thrive, and the child was unwanted. Only four percent of the cases involved battering.

Debruyn et al. (1992) studied a sample of children in the southwest of the United States. Abused children were matched with controls for age, sex, age, tribe and community. The abused children had parents (and grandparents) who abused drugs and alcohol more often, and more often had single parents, parents who had been arrested, and parents who had been raised in alcoholic families where domestic violence was common. The parents did not differ in being divorced. The abused and comparison children did not differ in whether there had been deaths in the family, whether they used drugs or whether they had been in trouble with the law. The abused children were, however, more often handicapped.

Causes

Among the many factors which have been suggested as causes of the abuse and neglect of Native American children include the absence of growing up in a well-functioning family by those Native Americans who were sent off to boarding schools or into foster care with white families for much of their own childhood. These boarding schools, and many of the foster homes, administered physical punishment, which modeled harsh discipline as a way of coping with children (Hull, 1982) and alienated the students from their culture. In addition, there may have been considerable sexual abuse of children in the boarding schools (Horejsi et al., 1992). Compounding the problem is the high rate of births to young, teenage, mothers whose parenting skills may be poor (Horejsi et al., 1992).

The erosion of traditional family networks in Native American communities, the unemployment and poverty, and the growing sense of isolation from the past are seen as the kinds of conditions that can increase the risk of child abuse (Fischler, 1985). Alcohol abuse, depression and suicidal behavior are common on some reservations, and these conditions also increase the risk of child abuse.

Finally, Fischler noted that some Native Americans have folk beliefs that make child abuse more likely. They may view children as possessing evil properties and seek help from a medicine man. Handicaps in children may be viewed as stemming from the parents violating cultural taboos, and the crippled child may be a constant reminder of these parental transgressions and a source of shame.

Comment

Horejsi et al. (1992) noted that parents investigated for child abuse and neglect often are uncooperative and hostile and may even leave the area after their children are removed from their care, apparently abandoning them. Horejsi noted that Native Americans have had much experience with oppressive white agencies and, based on past experience in their tribe, may believe that, once their children are removed from their care, they are gone for good. Thus, their children are "dead" for them.

Tribal communities are much like small towns, in which everyone knows everyone else's business. As a consequence, an investigation for child abuse and neglect soon becomes common knowledge, and the parents being investigated often feel acute shame and embarrassment, making them more likely to be uncooperative with authorities and more likely to flee the community.

Furthermore, their resistance to social workers and criminal justice workers may result, not only from their distrust of white agencies, but also from the very different communication style of Native Americans as compared to whites. These problems may be exacerbated by the alcohol and drug abuse in the parents.

Not only is child abuse a crime in itself, but the experience of abuse and neglect by children will impede their normal development, increasing the risk that they will become juvenile delinquents and criminals, alcohol and drug abusers and child abusers themselves as they try to cope with the resulting feelings of anger, hostility, depression and isolation (Berlin, 1987). Thus, it is crucial for child abuse and neglect to be addressed among Native Americans.

This issue has been relatively well-researched as compared to other issues related to Native American criminal behavior, but much more needs to be done, especially research comparing abuse and neglect among Native Americans living on reservations and those living in the general community and research on the causes of child abuse and neglect which would suggest tactics which might be useful in preventing child abuse and neglect.

REFERENCES

Berlin, I. N. Effects of changing Native American cultures on child development. *Journal of Community Psychology*, 1987, *15*, 299-306.

Blum, R. W., Harman, B., Harris, L., Bergeisen, L., & Resnick, M. D. American Indian-Alaska Native youth health. *Journal of the American Medical Association*, 1992, *267*, 1637-1644.

Carter, I., & Parker, L. J. Intrafamilial sexual abuse in American Indian families. In M. Q. Patton (Ed.), *Family sexual abuse*, pp. 106-117. Newbury Park, CA: Sage, 1991.

Debruyn, L. M., Lujan, C. C., & May, P. A. A comparative study of abused and neglected American Indian children in the southwest. *Social Science & Medicine*, 1992, *35*, 305-315.

Dietrich, G. Indian Child Welfare Act. *Child Abuse & Neglect*, 1986, *2*, 125-128.

Fischer, M. Adolescent adjustment after incest. *School Psychology International*, 1983, *4*, 217-222.

Fischler, R. S. Child abuse and neglect in American Indian communities. *Child Abuse & Neglect*, 1985, *9*, 95-106.

French, L. A. *The winds of injustice.* New York: Garland, 1994.

Horejsi, C., Craig, B. H. R., & Pablo, J. Reactions by Native American parents to child protection agencies. *Child Welfare*, 1992, *71*, 329-342.

Hull, G. H. Child welfare services to Native Americans. *Social Casework*, 1982, *63*, 340-347.

Long, K. A. Cultural considerations in the assessment and treatment of intrafamilial abuse. *American Journal of Orthopsychiatry*, 1986, *56*, 131-136.

Lujan, C., DeBruyn, L. M., May, P. A., & Bird, M. E. Profile of abused and neglected American Indian children in the southwest. *Child Abuse & Neglect*, 1989, *13*, 449-461.

Nagi, S. Z. *Child maltreatment in the United States.* New York: Columbia University Press, 1977.

Oakland, L., & Kane, R. The working mother and child neglect on the Navajo reservation. *Pediatrics*, 1973, *51*, 849-853.

Piasecki, J. M., Manson, S. M., Biernoff, M. P., Hiat, A. B., Taylor, S. S., & Bechtold, D. W. Abuse and neglect of American Indian children. *American Indian & Alaska Native Mental Health Research*, 1989, *3*, 43-62.

Robin, R. W., Chester, B., Rasmussen, J. K., Jaranson, J. M., & Goldman, D. Prevalence, characteristics, and impact of childhood sexual abuse in a southwestern American Indian tribe. *Child Abuse & Neglect,* 1997, *21,* 769-787.

Rowell, R. M., & Kusterer, H. Care of HIV infected Native American substance abusers. *Journal of Chemical Dependency Treatment,* 1991, *4*(2), 91-103.

White, R. B., & Cornely, D. A. Navajo child abuse and neglect study. *Child Abuse & Neglect,* 1981, *5,* 9-17.

Wichlacz, C. R., Lane, J. M., & Kempe, H. Indian child welfare. *Child Abuse & Neglect,* 1978, *2,* 29-35.

Wichlacz, C. R., & Wechsler, J. G. American Indian law on child abuse and neglect. *Child Abuse & Neglect,* 1983, *7,* 347-350.

Chapter 7

OTHER CRIMINAL BEHAVIORS

There are many areas of criminal behavior involving Native Americans which have received little examination by scholars. This chapter will briefly review what little is known about some of these areas.

Spouse Abuse

Spouse abuse is reported to be common among Native Americans, and scholarly reports are slowly beginning to appear on this issue.

Norton and Manson (1995) interviewed sixteen battered women seen for counseling at an urban Native American health center. The majority of these women were in their 20s, unemployed, with family incomes below $10,000. Half had children under the age of five at home, and five were pregnant. Thirty-eight percent of the women and 19 percent of the male abusers had injuries severe enough to warrant a visit to a physician. In the previous year, 38 percent of the women had experienced marital rape, and another 12 percent had experienced attempted rape by their partners. Most of the male abusers were drunk at the time, as were 62 percent of the women.

In a broader survey of Native American women, those reporting domestic violence did not differ from the others in age, education, number of children, employment or income. Abused women were more likely to be divorced or separated and reported more problems with alcohol than non-abused women.

Feinman (1992) noted that women played a major role in traditional Navajo culture. The society was matrilineal, matrilocal and matriarchal. Women controlled the land, owned the sheep, and participated in all aspects of Navajo life. After 1868, when the Navajo were conquered and confined to the reservation, the society was forced to accept Anglo values, laws and institutions, and this led to the devaluation of women as the society became "masculinized." The United States gave Navajo men the right to vote in 1924, four years before giving Navajo women the same right. The United States government used the men's family names to identify families, ordered the slaughter of the sheep, created jobs for men, and sent the children off to boarding schools to Americanize them. Thus, Navajo women were forced into the same low status vis-à-vis men as were white women. The influence of Anglo movies and television also increased the acceptability of violence.

In traditional Navajo culture, victims and wrongdoers are brought together with kin to resolve problems. Modern Navajo are often isolated from their culture, making such ceremonies impossible. Yet they distrust Anglo systems for dealing with these problems. Hospital and criminal justice personnel are often Navajo who belong to the woman's or the man's family or clan, and criticizing members of one's clan is not proper. Furthermore, confiding in these people may lead to the widespread dissemination of news about the battering. Federal law enforcement agencies do not like to handle battering cases, handing them over to the Navajo justice system, in which violence against women is not a specific crime and, therefore, has few provisions for helping battered women.

Help for battered Navajo women began in 1977 when the New Mexico Commission on the Status of Women held a workshop in Shiprock at the request of two Navajo women, a tribal lawyer and a former Navajo council delegate. A women's shelter opened in a trailer in January 1979 and moved to a permanent building in January 1985. The shelter has a capacity for 20 women and children, with eight bedrooms and a dormitory. It is supported with funds raised by the local Methodist church.

Brodribb (1988) describes the attempts by the Northern Indian Women's Association (NIWA) to set up a shelter for battered and unwed Canadian women of all ethnicities in 1975 in Ontario (Canada). Although the shelter was established, efforts to obtain funding from government agencies led to pressure to include other social service agencies in its development, displacing NIWA from its central position, turning it more into a coordinating agency. After four years of negotiations, the shelter was opened in 1980, with the Native

Canadian women feeling that their efforts had been preempted. The style of the service reflected the standard government polices rather than meeting the needs of women. The evaluation procedures for the shelter examined whether the shelter had met objectives which the Native Canadian women had been coerced into accepting. In 1980, only one Native Canadian woman attended board meetings, and five years later all the Native Canadian women had resigned. Brodribb noted that, not only was the shelter appropriated by non-Natives, but that the Native Canadian women received no support from Native Canadian men in their efforts.

There is hope for the future. Durst (1991) surveyed two Arctic communities, and respondents in both felt that now they would be more likely to actively intervene in cases of spouse abuse than they would ten years earlier. Thus, perhaps Native American communities will be more willing to address the issue of domestic violence in the future.

Victimization

There are few data available on the victimization of Native Americans. As Flowers (1990) has pointed out, Native Americans are grouped together with all other ethnic groups except whites and blacks in the national crime surveys, and so victimization rates cannot be calculated for Native Americans.

In the only study of victimization that could be located, Westermeyer and Peake (1983) followed up 45 Native American alcoholics ten years later and found that nine were deceased, three of whom were murdered, including one beaten to death in the course of being robbed.

Studies of victimization are urgently needed, both for Native Americans living on reservations and for those dwelling in the general community.

White-Collar Crime

White-collar crime is common on Native American reservations, although little research has appeared on the topic. For example, on the Standing Rock Sioux Reservation in South and North Dakota, Montaigne (1989) noted that many Native Americans who receive free food from the federal government then sell it to whites on the black market, usually for money with which to buy alcohol.

Montaigne noted that the tribal leaders squander much of the federal money given to them to run the reservation. An inn was built for $2.3 million and opened in 1973. Tribal councilman ran up large unpaid bar bills and packed the payroll with relatives and friends. The inn closed in 1977.

In 1984, outside companies conducting business on the reservation were taxed to provide a fund to create new businesses and jobs for tribal members. Over $200,000 was collected, over half of which was used to pay for vacations for tribal leaders while the rest was spent on administration. In 1987 alone, 17 tribal council members spent $430,00 on travel, most of which were junkets. Montaigne documented that tribal members billed for travel by car for trips on which they were actually passengers. They used their annual $5,000 fund for emergencies as gifts for relatives and friends.

Anon (1989) noted that the leader of the Navajo nation was investigated for corruption in office and was driven from office by the tribal council.

Gangs

De Witt (1998) noted that Native Americans youth are increasingly joining gangs, and he observed gang activity in the Pine Ridge Indian Reservation and in the Native American community in Rapid City (SD). He also suggested that the gangs may be involved in drug dealing, but he presented no documentation of this.

Tousey (1998) documented the growth of two gangs on the Menominee Indian Reservation in Keshena, Wisconsin, the Almighty Latin Kings and the Gangster Disciples, although several rival gangs have now established themselves on the reservation. He noted their growing involvement in drug dealing and burglaries and the increase in beatings, assaults and drive-by shootings as the gang members fought over turf.

Gangs have also been reported among rural Native American youths (Miller and Caulkins, 1964; Riffenburgh, 1964), urban Native American youths (Howard, 1970; White, 1970) and Native Canadian youth (Lewis, 1970; Price, 1964).

More research is needed on the extent of criminal behavior of these gangs and studies on the characteristics and motivations of those who join these gangs as compared to those who do not.

Drug Offenses

We have seen above that substance abuse is common among Native Americans. For example, in a survey of Native American students at a post-high school institution, 95 percent had tried beer, 70 percent marijuana, 36 percent amphetamines, 31 percent inhalants, 22 percent barbiturates, 21 percent hallucinogens, 13 percent cocaine, and 6 percent heroin (Goldstein et al., 1979).

Despite this, and despite the zealous activity of the Drug Enforcement Administration, there has ben little research into the manufacture and selling of illegal drugs by Native Americans.

Organized Crime

There is some evidence that organized crime has infiltrated the gambling facilities on Native American reservations. For example, Navajo gambling (such as bingo) was, and may still be, possibly controlled by the Mafia (Anon, 1989).

Environmental Crime

There are criminal aspects to the dumping of toxic wastes on Native American land and the exploitation of their mineral and water sources (French, 1994).

Political Crimes

In 1979, seven international jurists investigated whether there were political prisoners in the United States. They identified four categories of political prisoners, two of which involved Native Americans.[1]

(1) Victims of FBI misconduct and other forms of illegal government conduct. There was some criminal activity on both sides associ-

---

1. The other two categories were persons convicted of crimes committed in order to advance their political beliefs and persons who are arbitrarily selected for arrest because of their racial or economic status.

ated with the Native American protest movements, such as the confrontations between American Indian Movement (AIM) and the federal authorities in the 1970s (French, 1994).[2]

(2) Persons who, after imprisonment, become advocates for prison reform, for which they are punished (Mann, 1993).

Comment

It can be seen that there are many areas of criminal behavior among Native Americans which have been neglected both by researchers and by service providers. It is critical that the these areas be explored in the future.

REFERENCES

Anon. In the red. *The Economist*, 1989, February 25, 25-26.

Brodribb, S. Winonah's. *Resources for Feminist Research*, 1988, *17*(3), 49-55.

De Witt, D. C. Gang infiltration on the Pine Ridge Indian Reservation. *Official Proceedings of the 1998 Second International Gang Specialist Training Conference, volume 2*, pp. 37-44. Chicago: National Gang Crime Research Center, 1998.

Durst, D. Conjugal violence. *Community Mental Health Journal*, 1991, *27*, 359-373.

Feinman, C. Women battering on the Navajo reservation. *International Review of Victimology*, 1992, *2*, 137-146.

Flowers, R. B. *Minorities and criminality*. Westport, CT: Greenwood, 1990.

French, L. A. *The winds of injustice*. New York: Garland, 1994.

Goldstein, G. S., Oetting, E. R., Edwards, R., & Garcia-Mason, V. Drug use among Native American young adults. *International Journal of the Addictions*, 1979, *14*, 855-860.

Howard, J. H. Comment. *Current Anthropology*, 1970, *11*, 448-449.

Lewis, C. *Indian families on the northwest coast*. Chicago: University of Chicago, 1970.

Mann, C. R. *Unequal justice*. Bloomington, IN: Indiana University, 1993.

Messerschmidt, J. *The trial of Leonard Peltier*. Boston: South End Press, 1983.

Miller, F., & Caulkins, D. Chippewa adolescents. *Human Organization*, 1964, *23*, 150-159.

Montaigne, F. A shared disgrace. *The Philadelphia Inquirer Magazine*, 1989, February 26, 22-30, 35, 43.

Norton, I. M., & Manson, S. M. A silent minority. *Journal of Family Violence*, 1995, *10*, 307-318.

---

2. For an account of the AIM confrontation with FBI agents which resulted in the death of two FBI agents during a firefight and the trial and conviction of Leonard Peltier for the murder see Messerschmidt (1983).

Price, J. The urban integration of Canadian Native people. *Western Canadian Journal of Anthropology*, 1974, *4*, 29-47.

Riffenburgh, A. S. Cultural influences and crime among Indian Americans. *Federal Probation*, 1964, *28*(3), 38-46

Tousey, T. F. Training materials. *Official Proceedings of the 1998 Second International Gang Specialist Training Conference, volume 2*, pp. 119-153. Chicago: National Gang Crime Research Center, 1998.

Westermeyer, J., & Peake, E. A ten-year follow-up of alcoholic Native Americans in Minnesota. *American Journal of Psychiatry*, 1983, *140*, 189-194.

White, R. A. The lower class culture of excitement among the contemporary Sioux. In E. Nurge (Ed.), *The modern Sioux*, pp. 175-197. Lincoln, NE: University of Nebraska, 1970.

Part 3

THEORIES OF NATIVE AMERICAN CRIMINAL BEHAVIOR

Chapter 8

GENERAL THEORIES

May (1982) has summarized the major theories proposed to explain Native American criminal behavior. Some theories focus on the individual.

(1) Native Americans are inherently a more criminal group. We will address this issue in Chapter 9.

(2) Native Americans have high recidivism rates which leads to an inflation of the crime estimates for all Native Americans. There is very little research on this possibility.

Wormith and Goldstone (1984) studied inmates released from Canadian federal penitentiaries in three prairie provinces during a seven-month period. Each inmate was rated for a recidivism prediction score using a 15-item test developed on a sample of 2,500 inmates (Nuffield, 1982). Native Canadian inmates received significantly higher scores than non-Natives, predicting higher recidivism rates for them. The results are poorly presented in the report, but it appears that Native Canadians also recidivated more than non-Natives. However, the authors failed to use a regression analysis to explore whether race was a predictive factor after other factors were taken into account (such as age at release, offense type, and marital status).

Randall and Randall (1978) noted that parole failure rates were higher for Native Americans than for whites or blacks both in the Federal prison system from 1970 to 1972 (43% versus 28% and 33%, respectively) and in the Washington prison system from 1957 to 1959 (47% versus 38% and 34%).

Winfree and Griffiths (1975) studied the parole success of inmates released from a maximum security prison between 1966 and 1971, followed-up until 1972. The predictors of parole success were similar for Native Americans and non-Native Americans, with success associated with fewer prior convictions, more prior paroles, not being enrolled in the prison school (only the most poorly educated enrolled in the prison school), less time served, and moving in with their families after release. The one difference was that level of education did not predict parole success in the Native Americans while it did for the non-Native Americans.

Thus, the little research that there is supports the possibility that Native Americans may have higher rates of recidivism than other ethnic groups.

Other theories focus on the society.

(3) Adjustment as a result of acculturation may play a role (see also Flowers, 1990). Reasons (1972) noted the possible role of culture conflict, including the clash of cultures, the imposition of Anglo laws on Native American culture, and the migration of one culture into another. Petterson (1972) suggested that Native American youth face the dilemma of assimilating into Anglo culture or fighting for more self-determination, a conflict also reflected over the centuries in the federal policies toward Native Americans. This conflict between assimilation and self-determination is reflected in the educational system. Mission schools were replaced by boarding schools, both systems trying to force Native Americans to assimilate. These systems led to high dropout rates, poor educational achievement, poor job skills and poor employment prospects. The boarding schools were often used as dumping grounds for problem youths, and these adolescents sometimes exerted a bad influence on the other youths. More recently, there has been an effort to provide day schools with culturally sensitive material and Native American teachers.

(4) Social disorganization as a result of the historical trauma that Native Americans have experienced may contribute to the etiology of Native American criminal behavior. LaPrairie (1992) attributed the apparently high crime rate among Native Canadians to such factors as the erosion of traditional values (resulting in a lack of respect for others and an absence of shame among other things), the reservation system, and poverty. Poverty has also been proposed as an important causal element by Flowers (1990).

Ackerman (1971) studying the Nez Perces in Idaho pointed to the decline in patrilocality, communal discipline[1] and the traditional male and females roles, all of which served to better socialize the young in the past.

Minnis (1962) focused on the lack of land ownership in the tribe that she studied. In this tribe, the land had been fractionalized when assigned to families, and the subsequent inheritances had split up the land still further. Often people did not know which plots of land they owned, and much of it was too small or unproductive to farm. Many of the young adults were simply waiting around for elders to die and pass on the land to them.

(5) The social organization of Native American tribes may have resulted in varying levels of crime. For example, a tribe which places low value on property possession will have a low rate of property crime. We have seen in Chapter 5 that some scholars have suggested that current patterns of murder in Native American tribes are similar to the patterns found in the previous century and so are manifestations of traditional patterns of behavior.

(6) Native Americans demographically have a greater proportion of crime-prone individuals, such as young males. Interestingly, no research has appeared to test this possibility despite the clear evidence that rates of crime in the United States are strongly associated over time with the proportion of young males in the population.

Some theories focus on the criminal justice system.

(7) Native Americans are not a more criminal group, but their over-representation in the criminal justice system, is a result of racial discrimination by the criminal justice system (see also Flowers, 1990). We will address this possibility in Chapter 15.

(8) Native Americans are subjected to greater surveillance as a result of the many jurisdictions that have law enforcement powers over them —tribal, local, state and federal. Also, Native Americans utilize police more for minor matters than do members of other ethnic groups, which results in an inflation of police activity measures. Similarly, Petterson (1972) suggested that jurisdictional problems may lead to problem youths being subject to a variety of law enforcement agencies, with little chance for rational and consistent evaluations, dispositions and treatments.

---

1. She noted that Nez Perces parents and grandparents did not like to punish children physically, and so in the past punishment was carried out a by a community representative.

(9) Native Americans do not use the legal services available to gain lesser sentences. We will address this issue in Chapter 13.

We might add the following possibilities.

(10) Reasons (1972; see also Flowers, 1990) noted that alcohol use and abuse may play a role in Native American crime, especially the possibility that prohibition on many reservations prevents the development of norms for everyday self-regulated drinking. The role of alcohol in Native American crime was discussed in Chapter 4.

(11) Reasons (1972) noted that Native Americans may lack opportunities for legitimate means of obtaining valued goals, leading to the psychological state of anomie (see also Flowers, 1990; Minnis, 1962).

(12) Petterson (1972) noted that when the Native American community is granted and assumes responsibility for delinquent youth, the facilities are poor—little foster care, few alternatives to incarceration, poor probation and counseling services, no youth detention facilities, and no comprehensive plan to combat juvenile delinquency.

(13) Minnis (1962) suggested that family structure may play a role, such as high rates of illegitimate births, while Reasons (1972) suggested that economic factors such as poverty may play a role in Native American crime.

(14) It may be that the criminal and delinquent behavior of Native Americans is exaggerated. Garbarino (1971) observed that the delinquent behavior of Native American urban children and adolescents comprises mainly truancy or running away from home, behaviors he attributed to dislike of school, boredom and overcrowded conditions at home. As we have seen in Chapter 3, given the social status and age structure of Native Americans, their nonalcohol related crime rate is not high.

Comment

It is of interest to note that many of these possibilities, while frequently advanced as possible causes of criminal behavior in Native Americans, have generated little or no research to test their relevance. It is hoped that such research will be forthcoming in the future.

The next three chapters will present the major theories of criminal behavior and report the research on Native Americans which is relevant to the theories. There are two major theories of crime, however, for which there is no relevant research on Native Americans.

Classical Theories

The principles of the Classical School of criminology were stated most clearly by Cesare Beccaria (1738-1794) in Italy and Jeremy Bentham (1758-1832) in England. Beccaria, a mathematician and economist, was concerned about the inconsistencies in the ways governments managed various affairs. In criminal justice, it seemed to him, judges were capricious and swayed by personal considerations. Judges had considerable power in determining sentences and often added to the punishments prescribed by law.

In his book published in Italy in 1764, Beccaria (1963) argued that a system of laws and contracts is necessary for the society, but made by the legislature rather than the judges. The function of the judge should be simply to determine guilt, while the penalties should be a matter of law. He urged the establishment of a scale of crimes and punishments which takes into account only the criminal act itself and not the intent of the offender.

Beccaria saw punishment as useful for it prevents crime. Thus, laws should be published and learned well by the people, trials should be public and speedy, and punishment should be certain and immediate. In addition, he urged the end of torture, the use of imprisonment rather than capital punishment, and better conditions for prisons. Vold (1979) classifies Beccaria's position as legal and administrative criminology.

The ideas of Beccaria were based on several ideas current in social philosophy at the time. The idea of the *social contract* held that an individual was bound to society only by his consent and, therefore, society was responsible to the citizen as well as the reverse. Individuals had rights and should lose only enough liberty as to make society viable.

Behavior was also seen as the product of free will. It was purposive and determined by hedonism. People acted so as to maximize pleasure and minimize pain. Punishment, was therefore, intended to increase the pain resulting from criminal acts. This philosophy also did not admit of extenuating personal or social consequences to excuse the offender from punishment. The punishment should fit the crime, and Beccaria was not in favor of overly severe punishment. Punishment, if swift and certain, need be only as severe as necessary to deter people from criminal acts.

Meanwhile in England, Jeremy Bentham, a philosopher who also studied law, was also reflecting on crime and punishment (Bentham, 1967). Classified today as a *utilitarian hedonist,* Bentham wanted to maximize the good in the society–the greatest good for the greatest number of people. Like others in the eighteenth century, Bentham believed that people were rational and would choose to maximize pleasure and minimize pain.

Bentham, like Beccaria, proposed that specific punishments assigned to each crime would increase the pain and, thereby, decrease the incidence of crime. The potential pain of the criminal act when the offender is caught must outweigh the potential pleasure obtained. If this is so, then the rational person will refrain from committing the criminal act.

Like Beccaria, he also eschewed severe punishment, and he urged that only crimes which damage the society should be punished. Acts which are an offense only to morals and which do not interfere with the rights of others should not be considered criminal. Bentham also wrote on the design and management of prisons and served as an inspiration for a new type of prison administrator.

The classical position had a major impact on the criminal justice system for over a hundred years, but eventually it was replaced in the twentieth century by the view that criminals should be *treated* rather than *punished.* However, in recent years, the classical position has grown in strength again as efforts at rehabilitating criminals appear to have had little success (von Hirsch, 1976; Newman, 1983).

Modern classical theorists argue also for swift and certain punishments which do not necessarily have to be severe, punishments which are uniform and which fit the crime, and incapacitation of known chronic offenders so that they cannot commit additional crimes. Today we see many jurisdictions imposing fixed minimum terms for certain crimes (such as dealing drugs or crimes committed with a gun) and increasing incarceration rates (which is leading at the present time to overcrowded prisons).

Social Conflict Theories

Social conflict theories of crime focus on the ways that governments make and enforce laws both informally and formally. Might these laws simply be a way in which those in power maintain their power and control the oppressed in a society? Although this possibility has been proposed as a cause of criminal behavior in Native Americans, research to test its applicability is absent.

In this perspective laws and the criminal justice serve the interests of those in power. The criminal justice system oppresses those without power and status in the society and serves the interests only of those in power. The powerful seek to impose their conceptions of morality and their standards of behavior on the society and to protect their property and power. To do this, they are usually able to draw the middle classes into this pattern of control since maintenance of the control seems to serve middle-class interests as well.

According to this perspective, the poor, the lower classes and the oppressed do not commit more crimes than the oppressors. They are simply caught more often and punished more severely. Let us take a simple example which illustrates this.

Let us consider a poor lower-class citizen who takes a gun and robs a store owner of one thousand dollars. If caught he will be convicted of a felony and serve a long term in prison. Let us consider one of the firms that provides armaments for the Pentagon. We have read in recent years of the government being charged thousands of dollars for parts which can be bought in stores for a few dollars. We have read of companies found guilty of defrauding the government on contracts for millions of dollars. What happens to the owners of these companies? Nothing. The company may be fined, but that simply comes out of profits. The dividend to shareholders might be reduced by a few cents. Has the chief executive officer of any of those companies paid a fine out of his own pocket, let alone gone to prison? Of course not.

In the oil spill in Alaska in 1989, the highest-ranking person in Exxon sentenced so far in court has been the captain of the ship. To take a very different example, after the atrocities committed by Americans during their intervention in the civil war in Vietnam, the highest person charged and convicted was a lieutenant.

Most social conflict theorists of crime are Westerners, so they often attack the capitalist system in their theories. A social conflict theory of crime could be applied just as easily to communist dictatorships. Stalin and Brezhnev in the Soviet Union or Mao Zedong in the People's Republic of China were skilled in using the criminal justice system to maintain the status of the elite in power, despite supposedly having a

Marxist ideology at the basis of their system of government which is opposed to oppression.

Sykes (1974) has argued that the rules imposed by the ruling classes have little relationship to the cultural norms of the poor. In a society where affluence is well-publicized and becomes a major goal for people, frustration is bound to be generated in those who cannot attain and share in this affluence. The have-nots, therefore, develop a deep-rooted hostility toward the social order.

Schwendinger and Schwendinger (1979) argued that the legal system in the United States serves to secure an economic system that is centered around capitalism and guards the position of the owners at the expense of the workers. Many of the support systems, such as the education system, are designed to secure the labor force. Because of the antagonism built into the capitalist system, the legal system can never achieve its stated purpose of producing justice.

It is interesting to note that organizations set up to help the workers often become corrupted in their aims. The high levels of oppression in the so-called Marxist countries is good evidence of this. In our world, however, unions which initially did much to liberate the worker from abuse at the hands of the owners, eventually became rigid organizations whose leaders were often corrupt and who abused the workers they represented. In a more subtle diversion, union-run pension plans now invest their enormous funds in shares of the major companies, so that the well-being of the capitalists is tied to the well-being of the union workers and vice versa.

Quinney's (1970) conflict model is less tied to a critique of any particular governing system. Quinney suggested that crime is a definition of human conduct that is created by authorized agents in any politically organized society. These definitions describe behaviors that conflict with the interests of those segments of the society which shape public policy. The definitions are applied by those segments of the society which have the power to shape the criminal justice system. The less power your segment of society has, the greater the chance that your behavior patterns will be defined as criminal, and thus the greater the likelihood you will violate the criminal law.

Quinney suggested that conceptions of crime are diffused through the society by the channels of communication. This means that, today, those seeking to change the society often propose alternative definitions of crime and seek to diffuse these new definitions through the same communication channels. During America's intervention in the Vietnam civil war, antiwar groups defined those running the war as the real criminals. Ecology groups define industry as the real criminal. However, these redefinitions have to compete against those held by the majority and so are often disregarded, although in both examples given above the redefinitions eventually had a significant impact on the ruling segments of the society.

There is an important distinction between Marxist conflict theories and other conflict theories (Vold, 1979). In the Marxist perspective, criminal behavior may still be seen as pathological, but it is attributed to the pathological nature of capitalist society. Since the workers are denied a productive role in society, they become demoralized and act in criminal ways. If society was more socialist, the workers would less oppressed and criminal behavior would become less frequent. Other conflict criminologists, however, consider criminal behavior to be the normal actions of normal people who have insufficient power to control the criminalization process.

In the social conflict view, therefore, criminals are really "political criminals," and the solution to the crime problem is to reform the society. The oppression of one segment by another segment must be stopped and, unlike what has happened in previous attempts to do this, not simply replaced by alternative types of oppression. Social conflict theorists, therefore, would urge the elimination of racism, sexism, and other forms of oppression through a social revolution.

REFERENCES

Ackerman, L. A. Family instability and juvenile delinquency among the Nez Perces. *American Anthropologist*, 1971, *73*, 595-603.

Beccaria, C. *On crimes and punishments*. Translated by H. Paolucci. Indianapolis, IN: Bobbs-Merrill, 1963.

Bentham, J. *A fragment on government and an introduction to the principles of morals and legislation*. W. Harrison (Ed.). Oxford: Basil Blackwell, 1967.

Flowers, R. B. *Minorities and criminality*. Westport, CT: Greenwood, 1990.

Garbarino, M. S. Life in the city. In J. O. Waddell & O. M. Watson (Eds.), *The American Indian in urban society*, pp. 168-205. Boston: Little Brown, 1971.

LaPrairie, C. Aboriginal crime and justice. *Canadian Journal of Criminology*, 1992, *34*, 281-298.

May, P. A. Contemporary crime and the American Indian. *Plains Anthropologist*, 1982, *27*, 225-238.

Minnis, M. S. Selected social problems of Fort Hall Reservation. *Sociology & Social Research*, 1962, *46*, 436-445.

Newman, G. *Just and painful.* New York: Macmillan, 1983.

Nuffield, J. *Parole decision-making in Canada.* Ottawa: Ministry of Supply & Services, 1982.

Petterson, J. R. Education, jurisdictions, and inadequate facilities as causes of juvenile delinquency among Indians. *North Dakota Law Review*, 1972, *48*, 661-694.

Quinney, R. *The social reality of crime.* Boston: Little Brown, 1970.

Randall, A., & Randall, B. Criminal justice and the American Indian. *Indian Historian*, 1978, *11*(2), 42-48.

Reasons, C. Crime and the American Indian. In H. M. Bahr, B. A. Chadwick & R. C. Day (Eds.), *Native Americans today*, pp. 319-326. New York: Harper & Row, 1972.

Schwendinger, H., & Schwendinger, J. Delinquency and social reform. In L. Empey (Ed.), *Juvenile justice*, pp. 246-290. Charlottesville, VA: University of Virginia Press, 1979.

Sykes, G. The rise of critical criminology. *Journal of Criminal Law & Criminology*, 1974, *22*, 335-347.

Vold, G. B. *Theoretical criminology.* New York: Oxford University Press, 1979.

Von Hirsch, A. *Doing justice.* New York: Hill and Wang, 1976.

Winfree, T. L., & Griffiths, C. T. An examination of factors related to the parole survival of American Indians. *Plains Anthropologist*, 1975, *20*, 311-319.

Wormith, J. S., & Goldstone, C. S. The clinical and statistical prediction of recidivism. *Criminal Justice & Behavior*, 1984, *11*, 3-34.

Chapter 9

POSITIVIST INDIVIDUALISTIC THEORIES

The classical theory of crime reviewed in the previous chapter is one of the major *individualistic* theories of crime because it focuses on the individual criminal and how he might be deterred from engaging in criminal acts. Within a hundred years after the formulation of the classical theory of crime, people began to look at the physiological and psychological characteristics of criminals and the circumstances of their social milieu for an explanation of why people turn to criminal behavior. This *positivist* school rejected the emphasis on free will of the classical school in favor of determinism. They sought to identify the *causes* of criminal behavior using value-free scientific methods. In this chapter, we examine the individualistic approaches in this positivist school.

Physiological Explanations

The first major criminologist to suggest that criminals might have different physiological characteristics was an Italian physician Cesare Lombroso (1835-1909; Wolfgang, 1961). He felt that some individuals were 'born' criminals and could be identified by their physical appearance which he thought resembled man's evolutionary ancestors. Lombroso's ideas were developed by Raffaele Garofalo (1851-1934; Garofalo, 1968) and Enrico Ferri (1856-1929; Sellin, 1970) and attacked by Charles Goring (1970-1919; Goring, 1972).

One modern formulation of this school of thought has focused on whether there could be genetic basis for criminal behavior, and the studies of identical and nonidentical twins and of adopted children from criminal and noncriminal parents have provided some support for a genetic basis (Christiansen, 1977; Hutchings and Mednick, 1977).[1]

The association of physique with criminal behavior, proposed by Sheldon (1949), has received some support (Cortes and Gatti, 1972) although other investigators have reported a failure to find any association (McCandless et al., 1972).

Several investigators have studied possible biochemical causes of criminal behavior. Some of these investigations have focused on diet. For example, delinquents have been found to behave better in institutions if placed on a diet with reduced amounts of sugar (Schoenthaler and Doraz, 1983). Other investigators have explored the incidence of neurological dysfunction in delinquents. For example, habitually aggressive youths are found to have an increased incidence of abnormal electrical activity in their brains (Williams, 1969), while other investigators have reported a high incidence of learning disabilities in delinquents (Murray, 1976).

Research on Native Americans

There are some research studies which support the possibility of physiological differences between Native Americans and whites which may be relevant to criminal behavior, although the paucity of research makes any conclusions tentative at the present time.

Brooks and Reddon (1996) noted that testosterone levels in men are affected by a variety of factors (including age, biological rhythms, genetic factors, stress, life-style and diet). However, testosterone is also associated with aggression, with some research indicating that violent offenders have higher levels of testosterone than nonviolent offenders. Brooks and Reddon examined 194 male offenders seen at a psychiatric assessment unit for young offenders in Canada, between the ages of 15 and 17 who were white or Native. The Native youths were more likely to have committed violent crimes and less likely to have committed nonviolent crimes than the white youths (with no differences in the incidence of sexual crimes). Blood testosterone levels (taken in the morning) were higher in those committing violent crimes than in those committing nonviolent or sexual crimes. Testosterone levels were also

---

1. The possibility that a genetic defect involving an extra chromosome, the so-called XXY syndrome, might increase the likelihood of criminal behavior was not supported by research (Witkin, et al., 1976).

higher in the Native youth than in the white youth. The higher levels of testosterone in the Native youths was found for violent and for nonviolent offenses and for eleven of sixteen offenses (direct violence against person, indirect violence against person, robbery, threats, weapons, escape, property, fraud, motor vehicle, criminal negligence and alcohol/motor vehicle).[2]

In a follow-up study, Studer et al. (1997) studied testosterone levels of Native Canadian (mainly Cree) and white sex offenders in an inpatient sex offender treatment program. The two groups were matched roughly on age, physique and crime and had been on the same prison diet. However, the Native Canadians were younger, shorter, offended against older victims, had more prior nonsexual offenses, were less educated and had lower intelligence test scores. The Native Canadians had higher levels of testosterone and sex hormone binding globulin and lower levels of calcium and albumin after controls for age and body-mass index. However, in a comparison of Army enlistees, Ellis and Nyborg (1992) found no differences in blood testosterone levels between 49 Native Americans and 3,654 whites.

Early research reports suggested that Native Americans reacted physiologically to alcohol differently than do whites (e.g., Wolff, 1973), but Bennison and Li (1976) found no differences in ethanol metabolism between Native Americans and whites.

Psychological Approaches

There are many psychological approaches to the study of criminal behavior, with factors such as intelligence (Hirschi and Hindelang, 1977), extraversion combined with neuroticism (Eysenck, 1977) and the antisocial personality (Toch, 1979) proposed as correlates of criminal behavior.

Research On Native Americans

There are many studies on psychological similarities and differences between Native Americans and whites (e.g., Bruneau, 1984), but almost none of these studies are relevant to differences in criminal behavior.

---

2. The white youths had higher levels of testosterone for violence against property, nuisance, alcohol, drugs and sex.

Valliant et al. (1983) compared juvenile offenders and nonoffenders and found that Native Canadian nonoffenders obtained high scores on the MMPI scales for Psychopathic Deviate (Pd), Habitual Criminality and Authority Conflict and low scores on Intellectualization so that they resembled the Native American and white offenders more than the white nonoffenders.[3] This is the kind of research needed if the usefulness of a positivist individualistic theory of Native American crime is to be adequately evaluated.[4]

Comment

At the present time, there is no evidence that Native Americans and whites differ in psychological traits which might lead to differences in the frequency of criminal behavior. There is tentative evidence for differences in testosterone between the ethnic groups, but the research is in its early phases, and we cannot place confidence in the reliability of the differences until many more studies have been conducted on the issue.

REFERENCES

Bennison, L., & Li, T. K. Alcohol metabolism in American Indians and whites. *New England Journal of Medicine*, 1976, *294*, 9-13.

Brooks, J. H., & Reddon, J. R. Serum testosterone in violent and nonviolent offenders. *Journal of Clinical Psychology*, 1996, *52*, 475-483.

Bruneau, O. J. Comparison of behavioral characteristics and self-concepts of American Indian and Caucasian pre-schoolers. *Psychological Reports*, 1984, *54*, 571-574.

Christiansen, K. O. A review of studies of criminality among twins. In S. A. Mednick & K. O. Christiansen (Eds.), *Biosocial bases of criminal behavior*, pp. 45-88. New York: Gardner.

Cortes, J. B., & Gatti, F. M. *Delinquency and crime.* New York: Seminar, 1972.

Ellis, L., & Nyborg, H. Racial/ethnic variations in male testosterone levels. *Steroids*, 1992, *57*, 72-75.

---

3. Valliant noted that the MMPI may not be valid for Native Canadians since it was derived on white samples, but the use of standard psychological tests for Native Americans seems to be valid (Lester, 1997).

4. Incidentally, Mandelzys and Lane (1980) found that MMPI scores were not associated with offense severity, predicted recidivism, or criminal history for a sample of Native Canadian inmates. Compared to reported MMPI scores from other sample of inmates in North America, the Native Canadian inmates had higher scores only on scales F and Sc.

Eysenck, H. J. *Crime and personality.* London: Routledge & Kegan Paul, 1977.

Garofalo, R. *Criminology.* Translated by R. Miller. Montclair, NJ: Patterson Smith, 1968.

Goring, C. *The English convict.* Montclair, NJ: Patterson Smith, 1970.

Hirschi, T., & Hindelang, M. Intelligence and delinquency. *American Sociological Review,* 1977, *42,* 471-586.

Hutchings, B., & Mednick, S. A. Criminality in adoptees and their adoptive and biological parents. In S. A. Mednick & K. O. Christiansen (Eds.), *Biosocial bases of criminal behavior,* pp. 127-141. New York: Gardner, 1977.

Lester, D. *Suicide in American Indians.* Commack, NY: Nova Science, 1997.

Mandelzys, N., & Lane, E. B. The validity of the MMPI as it pertains to Canadian Native inmates. *Canadian Journal of Criminology,* 1980, *22,* 188-196.

McCandless, B. R., Persons, W. S., & Roberts, A. Perceived opportunity, delinquency, race and body build among delinquent youth. *Journal of Consulting & Clinical Psychology,* 1972, *38,* 281-283.

Murray, C. *The link between learning disabilities and juvenile delinquency.* Washington, DC: US Government Printing Office, 1976.

Schoenthaler, S., & Doraz, W. Diet and crime. *International Journal of Biosocial Research,* 1983, *4,* 29-39.

Sellin, T. Enrico Ferri. In H. Mannheim (Ed.), *Pioneers in criminology,* pp. 232-271. Montclair, NJ: Patterson Smith, 1970.

Sheldon, W. H. *Varieties of delinquent youth.* New York: Harper, 1949.

Studer, L. H., Reddon, J. R., & Siminoski, K. G. Serum testosterone in adult sex offenders. *Journal of Clinical Psychology,* 1997, *53,* 375-385.

Toch, H. *Psychology of crime and criminal justice.* New York: Holt, Rinhart & Winston, 1979.

Valliant, P. M., Asu, M. E., & Howitt, R. Cognitive styles of Caucasian and Native Indian juvenile offenders. *Psychological Reports,* 1983, *52,* 87-92.

Williams, D. Neural factors related to habitual aggression *Brain,* 1969, *92,* 503-520.

Witkin, H., Mednick, S., Schulsinger, F., Bakkestrom, E., Christiansen, K., Goodenough, D., Hirschhorn, K., Lundsteen, C., Owen, D., Philip, J., Rubin, D., & Stocking, M. Criminality in XYY and XXY men. *Science,* 1976, *193,* 547-555.

Wolff, P. H. Vasomotor sensitivity to alcohol in diverse Mongoloid populations. *American Journal of Genetics,* 1973, *15,* 193-199.

Wolfgang, M. E. Pioneers in criminology: Cesare Lombroso. *Journal of Criminal Law, Criminology, & Police Science,* 1961, *52,* 361-369.

Chapter 10

SOCIAL STRUCTURE THEORIES

There are several positivist theories of crime which focus on the social structure or organization of society as causative factors. Some of these theories focus on the destructive social forces which arise from the prevailing cultural norms and values existing in lower class culture and may be called *culture deviance theories*, while another set focuses upon the frustration felt by lower class youths when they are prevented from obtaining rewards in the legitimate sphere and may be called *strain theories*.

Culture Deviance Theory

If the cultural values of the people in the area you grow up in do not conform to those of the main society, then conformity to these deviant rules, values and norms will lead to deviant behavior.

Shaw and McKay (1972), studying Chicago in the 1920s, noted that the city had greatly differing neighborhoods. Some were marked by wealth and luxury while others were slums. Shaw and McKay argued that delinquency was caused by the conditions in these slum areas. Often teenage gangs developed in these neighborhoods, and these gangs assisted the youths to survive and provided economic gain and friendship. The gangs then served as cultural agents, transmitting the new norms and values to the younger kids as they grew up and joined the gangs.

Shaw and McKay documented differences in attitudes and values in the different neighborhoods in Chicago and different patterns of child rearing. Parents in the neighborhoods with low crime rates stressed the importance of school, church and other community organizations, and families were tight knit. In the neighborhoods with high crime rates, there was a conflict in the cultural values, rather than a homogeneous deviant culture. Some families continued to stress conventional values, while others rejected such values. The youths in these neighborhoods had to choose with which set of values to align themselves, and they often chose the deviant set of values.

Miller (1958) also explained crime and delinquency as a the result of lower class culture. He stressed the role of female-headed households with the absence of good male role models for the adolescents, and he felt that the absence of men facilitated the establishment of male gangs as a substitute. He also noted the importance of several focal concerns in this culture which become goals: getting into and staying out of trouble, recognition of physical and mental toughness, establishing an image of street-wise smartness, the search for excitement, a belief in fate and luck as determinants of outcomes in life, and a concern with personal freedom and autonomy. Youths who become delinquents and criminals do so by conforming to these cultural demands.

Sellin (1938) stressed the role of conflict in norms. He argued that every individual knows the right and wrong way to behave in situations. In the normal process of growing up and becoming socialized, these norms clash, leading to culture conflict. Primary conflict occurs when two different cultures conflict, while secondary conflict occurs within the development of a single culture. An immigrant to the United States who behaves according to the norms of his home country illustrates primary conflict. A conflict between the values of native-born lower-class youths and middle-class values illustrates secondary conflict, and it this type of conflict that is responsible for a high rate of crime.

Wolfgang and Ferracuti (1967) proposed a subcultural theory of crime which suggested that there was a subculture which had its own norms separate from those of the dominant culture. In particular, Wolfgang and Ferracuti suggested that a common subculture was one of violence especially among some groups of the population (such as younger men) and in some regions, such as the southern states of America (Lester, 1986-1987).

Strain Theory

Strain theories focus on the feelings of the those in different groups or subcultures in the society. If you are unable to achieve success, prestige or status through legitimate means, then it is likely that you will feel anger and frustration. Strain theories propose that we all share similar goals and values (a very different assumption from the cultural deviance theories), but that we differ in our ability to achieve these goals, especially if we come from the lower social classes.

Merton (1957) argued that social structures establish goals for the members of the society and approve some methods for obtaining these goals. Nonconforming behavior results when people reject either the goals or the means for obtaining the goals. Merton suggested that modern America emphasizes goals rather than means and that the most sought after goal is wealth and material goods.

He identified five methods or *modes* of adaptation available to members of the society. *Conformists* accept both the goals and the approved means to obtain them. *Innovators* accept the goals but reject the approved means, as when a youth steals a car. *Ritualists* reject the goals but accept the approved means and, therefore, go through the rituals without any fundamental commitment to the goals toward which they appear to be aiming. *Retreatists* reject both the goals and the approved means and are illustrated by psychotics, vagabonds and vagrants. *Rebels* not only reject both the goals and the approved means, but they set out to establish a new social order. It can be seen that criminals fall mainly into the innovator type.

Cohen (1955) argued that the criminal behavior in slum districts is really a protest against the norms and values of middle-class culture. The social conditions of the slums make it difficult, if not impossible, for the youths to obtain the approved goals by the approved methods. These youths experience frustration which results in nonutilitarian, malicious and negativistic behavior. Parents in these districts fail to teach their children the proper skills for entering into the middle class culture, and so their children lack educational and communication skills and are unable to delay gratification. They fail to measure up to the *middle-class measuring rods*.

There are three adaptational styles which result from this failure. The *college boy* does not give up but embraces the middle-class values and tries to be successful according to these values. The *stable corner-*

boy hangs out in the neighborhood, gambles, is truant from school, engages in athletics and eventually gets a menial job. He withdraws into the comfortable world of the lower class. The *delinquent boy* adapts by becoming a criminal.

Cloward and Ohlin (1960) added to these analyses by noting that not even illegitimate means for achieving goals are evenly distributed in the society. Some lower class neighborhoods provide more opportunities for getting into a criminal career. Youths who know adults already engaged in crime can enter the criminal subculture as apprentices. If the peer groups and the adults do not provide this criminal learning experience, then the youth may retreat into drug use or simply seek catharsis through violence.

Social Structure And Native American Crime

Even back in the 1940s, Hayner (1942) recognized that crime rates varied by reservation. He noted that Colville in the northwestern United States, an isolated community with modest economic resources, had a low crime rate. In contrast, Yakima, a community with more contact with whites and economic prosperity, had a high crime rate, while Klamath had the highest crime rate of the three communities and the most contact with whites and the most prosperity. Thus, Hayner concluded that Native American crime rates increased with prosperity and contact with whites.

Minnis (1963) studied 130 households of the Shoshone-Bannock living on the Fort Hall, Idaho, reservation. She documented, first of all, poverty on the reservation. For example, only 18 percent of the homes had a bathroom, and only 64 percent had electricity. She also noted a higher proportion of children and adolescents among the tribes as compared to the United States population overall.

Fifty-eight percent of the sample had a record of breaking the law during the period 1934 to 1960. The 130 households had a record of 527 offenses, with obviously a good deal of recidivism. In 1959, the arrest rate in Fort Hall was 161 per 100,000 as compared to 46 for the United States. The arrest rate appeared to have been rising during the 1950s. The majority of the offenses were misdemeanors, predominantly involving vagrancy, drunkenness and disorderly conduct. Auto theft was rare, probably because offenders are easily discovered by the tribal police officers and because adolescents have difficulty affording gasoline for the cars. Minnis found that the most-crowded households had members with less education, more welfare recipients and higher rates of criminal records.

Phillips and Inui (1986) attempted to explore the effect of acculturation stress on crime in Native Alaskans. However, rather than examining criminal behavior per se, they examined Native Alaskan and white offenders referred for mental health evaluations or treatment. These offenders may not be representative of offenders in general, and so it is hard to see the usefulness of the results reported.

Phillips and Inui examined 95 percent of the records for mentally ill criminal offenders from 1977 to 1981 in Alaska. Native Alaskans comprised Eskimos (8.5% of the total population, including Yupik and Inupiat-speaking groups), Native Americans (5.4% of the total population) and Aleuts (2.0% of the total population). The proportion of Native Alaskans in the Alaskan population fell from 50 percent in 1950 to 16 percent in 1980; the percentage living in communities of 1,000 or more rose from 4 percent to 43 percent; 43 percent of Native Alaskans had finished high school by 1980 and 49 percent were in the labor force (as compared to 82 percent and 75 percent of whites). Intermarriage was common, and 42 percent of Native Alaskan children born in 1977 to 1981 had one white parent.

For the period 1977-1981, Native Alaskans had a higher arrest rate than whites (8,303 per 100,000 versus 3,793), including a higher arrest rate for violent felonies (544 versus 167) and a higher rate of being murdered (25 versus 8). Native Alaskans who were arrested were more likely to be given a psychiatric referral than whites who were arrested.

For those offenders referred for to mental health staff, taking into account their proportions in the Alaskan population, Native Alaskans referrals did not differ in sex or age. Native Alaskans who had never been married were more likely to be referred than whites, as were Native Alaskans who had entered high school, but unemployed Native Alaskans were less likely to be referred than unemployed whites.

Native Alaskan referrals were more likely to be diagnosed with an alcohol-related disorder (and to be drunk at the time of the offense) and less likely to be diagnosed with personality disorder or adjustment disorder. There were no differences in other diagnoses. Native Alaskans who were referred were more likely to have been arrested for violent crimes and less likely for property crimes. They were not more likely to be convicted or receive longer sentences. The ethnic density of the region did not seem to be related to the rate of referral (or indeed to the overall arrest rate for criminal behavior), and regional variations seemed to be more important than ethnic variations.

Native Alaskans who had moved from rural to urban areas were more likely to be referred than those who had not experienced such a change. This final finding, perhaps a measure of acculturation stress, illustrates the problem with this study. Had this finding been shown to apply to all Native Alaskan offenders, we might be able to conclude that acculturation stress played a role in the causation of criminal behavior. But the data are only for those offenders referred for a psychiatric evaluation, and so we cannot draw such a conclusion.

LaPrairie (1988) classified Canadian reserves in the Province of Quebec into four types based on the levels of personal resources (employment and education opportunities off the reserve and social integration with the non-Native community) and institutional completeness (employment opportunities on the reserve, self-government, and Native-owned enterprises):

	Personal resources	Institutional completeness
inert	low	low
pluralistic	low	high
integrative	high	low
municipal	average	high

She found that violent crimes rates were highest in the pluralistic and municipal reserves (followed by the integrative and inert reserves) while property crime rates were highest in only the municipal reserves (followed by the pluralistic, integrative and inert reserves). Police service requests were also most frequent in the municipal reserves, followed by the integrative, inert and pluralistic. Thus, LaPrairie's study shows clearly the influence of community structure on crime rates.

Comment

The existence of gangs (see Chapter 8) in Native American communities and the impoverished conditions on some Native American reservations (see Chapter 2) suggests that social structure theories of crime may be applicability to Native American crime, especially the theories of Shaw and McKay and of Miller.

Minnis's research has documented the association of poverty with criminal behavior on Native American reservations. On the other hand, LaPrairie's research indicates the complexity of the problem since, in her study, reservations low and average in personal resources both had high violent crime rates while reservations average in personal resources had high property crime rates, indicating that the association may not be a simple linear one.

More research needs to be done on these issues, but this preliminary research indicates that social structure theories of crime may be useful in explaining crime on Native American reservations.

REFERENCES

Cloward, R., & Ohlin, L. *Delinquency and opportunity*. New York: Free Press, 1960.

Cohen, A. *Delinquent boys*. New York: Free Press, 1955.

Hayner, N. Variability in the criminal behavior of American Indians. *American Journal of Sociology*, 1942, *47*, 602-613.

LaPrairie, C. P. Community types, crime and police services on Canadian Indian reserves. *Journal of Research in Crime & Delinquency*, 1988, *25*, 375-391.

Merton, R. *Social theory and social structure*. Glencoe, IL: Free Press, 1957.

Miller, W. Lower class culture as a generating milieu of gang delinquency. *Journal of Social Issues*, 1958, *14*, 5-19.

Minnis, M. S. The relationship of the social structure of an Indian community to adult and juvenile delinquency. *Social Forces*, 1963, *41*, 395-403.

Phillips, M. R., & Inui, I. S. The interaction of mental illness, criminal behavior and culture. *Culture, Medicine & Psychiatry*, 1986, *10*, 123-149.

Sellin, T. *Culture, conflict, and crime*. New York: Social Science Research Council, 1938.

Shaw, C. R., & McKay, H. D. *Juvenile delinquency and urban areas*. Revised edition. Chicago: University of Chicago Press, 1972.

Wolfgang, M. E., & Ferracuti, F. *The subculture of violence*. London: Tavistock, 1967.

Chapter 11

SOCIAL PROCESS THEORIES

The theories discussed in the previous chapter proposed that the structure of the society was a primary cause of crime and delinquency. In contrast, the theories described in this chapter focus on *social processes*, the relationships between the individual and people in the society, such as parents, teachers, friends, and so on. Thus, these theories have a sociopsychological orientation, stressing such factors as the learning of criminal attitudes, feelings of alienation from society, and a poor self-concept.

There are three major types of social process theory. *Learning theories* hold that crime is learned from one's associates and friends. *Social control theory* holds that delinquency and crime are the result of disrupted ties between the individual and the major institutions of the society – family, peers and school. *Labeling theory* focuses on the labels that others in the society give to the individual who is misbehaving.

Learning Theories

Differential Association Theory

Sutherland (1947) proposed that criminal behavior was learned in interaction with other persons. People do not become criminals simply by living in a particular type of society. Criminal, and other deviant patterns of behavior, are actively learned by people from others who serve as teachers and guides. This learning occurs primarily within intimate personal groups. It is family members, friends, and peers who have the most influence.

The learning covers the techniques of committing the crime as well as the specific motives, drives, rationalizations and attitudes. (Thus, criminals come to hold different values and attitudes from those held by law-abiding people.) People have to be coached on how to pick a lock or shoplift, as well as learning how to react to their crimes and their victims. If more of the person's friends and family are violating the law rather than following the law, the balance is tipped in favor of the person becoming a law violator. Furthermore, the quality and intensity of the person's relationships with the potential teachers and guides is critical. The more durable relationships have more influence on the person, as do those that occur at a young age, and the prestige of the potential teacher increases the likelihood of learning.

Sutherland thought that the mechanisms for learning criminal behavior were no different from the mechanisms responsible for learning any behavior. As psychologists, we would expect classical conditioning, operant conditioning, imitation and modeling, and insight learning all to play a role.

Neutralization Theory

Sykes and Matza (1957; Matza, 1964) proposed a theory which has come to be known as *neutralization theory* or *drift theory*. They proposed that delinquents hold values and attitudes similar to those of law-abiding people, but they learn techniques which enable them to neutralize these values and attitudes temporarily when committing crimes. The potential criminal learns through his interactions with others to disregard the controlling influences of the society's social rules.

On a continuum from total freedom to total constraint, most people lie somewhere in the middle, but we can move toward one end or the other depending upon our state of mind or the social situation we are in. This movement is called drift. The delinquent subculture encourages drift toward the freedom end of the continuum, and it provides a set of justifications for the violations of law and order.

The techniques of neutralization include:

(1) Denial of responsibility–the act was not their fault or was due to forces beyond their control. "It wasn't my fault"

(2) Denial of criminal intent–they were not stealing, they were borrowing–or they did not mean to damage the property, they were simply playing. "I didn't mean to do it."

(3) Denigration of the victim–the crime may be justified by disparaging the victim–he was an offensive authority figure or a member

of an outgroup (such as a homosexual)—the owner of the property was absent. "He had it coming to him."

(4) Condemning the moral authorities—police are seen as brutal oppressors and judges as corrupt—teachers and parents are unfair. "Why pick on me? Politicians get away with it."

(5) Appealing to higher loyalties—seeing loyalty to their peer group as more important than following the rules of the larger society. "I had to help my buddy."

Native American Crime and Delinquency

Winfree et al. (1989) set out to explore the usefulness of social learning theory for explaining Native American delinquency. They felt that social learning theory was likely to apply to all cultures, unlike other theories of crime and delinquency. Culture may affect what is learned, but it is less likely to affect how it is learned (Akers, 1985).

The social learning theory of crime and delinquency proposed by Akers (1985) borrowed heavily from behavioral learning theory (Bandura, 1977) and differential association theory (Sutherland and Cressey, 1966). The theory uses four main constructs to account for criminal behavior: imitation, differential reinforcement, differential definitions, and differential associations.

Winfree tested the theory by surveying students in grades 6 through 12 in a single rural school district, obtaining self-reports of delinquent behavior from 113 Native American youths and 372 white youths. They studied self-reports of alcohol and marijuana use in the previous 12 months, actions which technically were illegal since the youths were under the age of 18 and marijuana possession at the time of the study was a violation of state law. Native Americans and whites had used alcohol with the same frequency, but more Native Americans had used marijuana.

Winfree measured differential association by asking about the students' perception of the level of usage by their peers and differential definitions by asking the students how they felt about the use of alcohol and marijuana and how many discussions (positive and negative) they had with close friends and parents about usage.

For alcohol, the use by best friends and the students' own personal definitions predicted usage for both Native American and white youth.

For the white youths, peer opinions about usage also predicted usage. For marijuana, all four predictor variables predicted usage for both Native American and white youths: personal opinions, peer opinions, parent opinions and usage by best friends.

Winfree concluded that social learning was effective is explaining these status offenses in both Native American and white youths. This promising study on drug use needs to be extended to delinquent behaviors, so that the usefulness of a learning theory of crime can be evaluated.

Social Control Theories

The second major type of social process theory of criminal behavior focuses on the ties between the individual on the one hand and conventional groups in the society, other law-abiding individuals, and the organizations and institutions of the society on the other. Those who have close relationships with parents, friends, and teachers are more likely to have a positive self-image and to be able to resist the temptation of crime. Those who feel detached from conventional society are unaffected by its social control functions. These theories are usually called *social control theories.*

The social controls may be internal or external. Internal controls involve such personality traits as a positive self-image and a strong internalized conscience. External controls involve positive close relationships with parents and with teachers who are conventional and law-abiding.

Social Bond Theory

Hirschi (1969) assumed that all of us are potential criminals and that only social controls, not moral values, prevent us from behaving in a criminal manner. Hirschi noted four elements in the social bond between the individual and society.

(1) *Attachment* refers to the individual's interest in, sensitivity to, and caring for others, as well as concern for the wishes and expectations of others. The norms and values of the society are shared by the members and, if one cares about the reactions of others, then there is good reason to follow the norms.

Attachment to parents is the most important tie. If parents divorce or if one or both parents behave in such a way (abusively, for example) that the child's tie to them is weakened, then attachment will not take place. Without attachment to these first important people in our life, our parents, it is unlikely that the person will develop feelings of respect for others.

(2) *Commitment* refers to the time, energy and effort in pursuing conventional goals in our society. If the individual has a stake in the society, then behaving deviantly endangers this. For example, if the person pursues an education, obtains a good job, seeks prestige and status, and becomes a property owner, then he will be less likely to engage in criminal behavior because that would jeopardize his position in the society.

(3) A person who is *involved* in conventional activities in the society not only has less desire to engage in criminal behavior, but he also has less time.

(4) Finally the social bond involves *belief* in the moral validity of the norms established by the society for himself. Those norms must be seen as both good and correct for the society and as relevant to our own actions.

Hirschi found that high school students who felt close to their parents were less likely to engage in delinquent acts. Similarly, those who enjoyed and were successful in school were less likely to commit delinquent acts. Attachment to peers was also related, though less strongly, to avoidance of delinquent behavior. Students with high educational and occupational aspirations were less likely to commit delinquent acts, as were those who spent more time in conventional activities such as homework. Finally, those students who had committed delinquent acts were just as likely to accept middle-class values as the students who avoided delinquent acts. Thus, the delinquent students held conventional values but apparently did not see the relevance of these values for themselves.

Two important findings from Hirschi's research were that the delinquent groups rarely recruited "good" boys and influenced them to turn bad and, secondly, that the delinquents did not have particularly warm or intimate relationships with one another.

Containment Theory

Reckless (1967) focussed on internal controls as well as external controls. He noted that there were both pressures toward delinquency and away from it.

(1) **Inner containments** consisted of those forces in the personality resisting criminal involvement. People with a positive self-image, a strong ego, high frustration tolerance, goal orientation, and the ability to reduce tension in socially acceptable ways are less likely to engage in criminal behavior.

(2) **Outer containments** are those normative rules and values that society possesses which restrain antisocial and criminal behavior. People with a sense of belonging, who are effectively supervised and disciplined, and who have a meaningful social role are less likely to commit criminal acts.

(3) **Internal pushes** are those forces within the individual which propel him toward criminal behavior, such as restlessness, hostility, rebellion, internal conflicts, and the need for immediate gratification.

(4) **External pulls** are those forces in the society which pull the individual toward criminal acts such as deviant companions and the mass media.

(5) **External pressures** are those adverse social conditions which increase the likelihood of deviant behavior, such as poverty, unemployment, minority status, and limited opportunities.

Reckless proposed that the internal containments were more important than the external containments since we spend most of our time away from our family and the other groups supportive of the social order. We have to rely most of the time, then, on our internal strengths to control our criminal impulses.

Native American Crime and Delinquency

Robbins (1984) tried to test Hirschi's social control theory with the Seminole youth living on three Native American reservations in Florida (Hollywood, Big Cypress and Brighton). She surveyed 129 youths between the ages of ten and seventeen, about 70 percent of all of the youths on the reservations.

The percentages on the three reservations reporting one or more delinquent acts ranged from 59.5 percent to 81.8 percent. Males reported more delinquent acts, but age was unrelated to the frequency of such acts. Interestingly, the youths refused to answer questions about the delinquent acts of others–they responded to such questions by checking the "don't know" and "no response" answers. In Seminole culture, it is clearly appropriate to confess to one's own actions but not to report on the actions of others.

Robbins failed in her measure of attachment to family. Hirschi's suggested indices were inappropriate for the Seminole youths. Concepts such as "intimacy of communication" had little meaning for the youths. Seminole families do not communicate much at this level, yet everyone knows that he or she is loved.

Measures of attachment to non-Native American persons and institutions (teachers, school and the police) were associated with self-reported delinquency. Three of the nine associations were statistically significant. The associations were stronger in Hollywood than in Big Cypress and Brighton. In general, then, Seminole youths who respected the police, liked school and cared what their teachers thought about them were less likely to be involved in delinquent behavior.

In a follow-up analysis of these data, Robbins (1985) tired to measure commitment and belief in these adolescents. Commitment was measured by their responses to such questions about whether they thought they would get caught after delinquent acts and how much trouble they would get into. Belief was measured by questions on whether they would feel guilty after delinquent acts.

The majority of the adolescents believed that they would get caught and that their parents would find out. However, they did not think that they would get into much trouble. The majority also believed that delinquent acts were wrong. Those who believed that the acts were wrong were less likely to report having committed delinquent acts than those who did not believe that the acts were wrong.

In each of the three reservations, involvement in delinquent acts was predicted by commitment and belief, although Robbins interpreted her results as indicating that external controls were stronger than internal controls.[1]

Robbins expected the rate of self-reported delinquency to be highest in the more urban reservations, and the rate was higher in Hollywood and Big Cypress than in Brighton, the most geographical-

---

1. Her data analysis was rather simple and inadequate for drawing sound conclusions from her data.

ly isolated. Hollywood is the most urban reservation, while Big
Cypress, although rural, has encouraged commercial enterprise on the
reservation. Robbins's study, then, provides some support for social
control theories of crime on Native American reservations.

Social Reaction Theories

Social reaction theory is more commonly known as *labeling theory*. It
focuses upon how other people in the society react toward the delinquent. Most kids break the rules of the society at one time or another,
and many break the laws. A few of these kids get labeled. Some may
be labeled by their parents, relatives, friends and teachers—"You're
going to grow up and come to no good," "You are evil," and similar
statements. Others will get formally processed by the criminal justice
system and officially called juvenile delinquents. Social reaction theory focuses upon this informal and formal labeling process.

A person may be called many things as they grow up. For social
reaction theory, there is sometimes a point at which the adolescent
decides that a particular label is appropriate and accepts it. Once the
label is accepted, then the person has truly entered on a "career."

The social reaction perspective draws our attention to the audience,
to those who label others. It is clear that labeling is culturally determined. What is unlawful in one society or in one group within a society may be acceptable in another. For example, bribery of public officials is punishable in some societies while considered the norm in others. Sexually promiscuous behavior is considered a delinquent behavior in American girls but not in American boys.

Social reaction theory, therefore, focuses on discrimination in the
criminal justice system. Middle-class offenders are less likely to be
labeled and less likely to be severely punished than lower-class offenders. African Americans and Native Americans may be treated differently than whites (see Chapter 15), and females treated differently than
males.

Social reaction theory also inquires into the stigma of labels. The
labels are usually quite long-lasting and involve a loss of status. The
labeled person becomes a social outcast. This in turn leads to alienation from the mainstream of the society and makes continuation of a
criminal career even more likely. If you are an "X," then it is more

pleasant to seek the company of others who are also labeled "X's." Thus, labeling leads to the development of a new deviant identity and deviant subcultures. Individuals become what the society says they are.

Lemert (1967) distinguished between primary and secondary deviance. Primary deviance is deviant behavior which is accepted by others. For example, a person may behave antisocially at a party when drunk. The behavior may be excused because the party constitutes a "time-out" from the rules of society and because the person was drunk. Primary deviance goes unlabeled by others and by the self.

However, some deviant behavior, especially if it is frequent or becomes organized into a role (or a career), becomes recognized as such and labeled by others and, eventually, the self. This is secondary deviance.

Becker (1963) classified people as either behaving deviantly or conventionally and being labeled as deviant or ignored, giving four types:

(1) The *conformist* behaves conventionally and is not labeled.

(2) The *falsely accused* behaves conventionally but gets labeled as deviant anyway.

(3) The *pure deviant* behaves in a deviant manner and gets so labeled.

(4) The *secret deviant* behaves in a deviant manner but does not get labeled, perhaps because people are not aware of the deviant behavior.

The Social reaction theory has generated a great deal of research into the criminal justice system, especially on police discretion, prosecutorial decisions and sentencing, since these are the stages where labeling can take place. For example, when a police officer apprehends a suspect, he can let the youth go home with a warning or he can take him in and record the crime. This is the crucial first decision point in the criminal justice system.

The treatment implications of social reaction theory have centered around diversion (Schur, 1973). In diversion, efforts are made to keep youths out of the criminal justice system, especially if their crimes are minor. Such youths can be sent instead to community clinics, foster homes, job training or recreational programs, or educational programs. This would lessen the chances of them being labeled as delinquents and so deciding to enter a criminal career.

Native Americans and Labeling

In Chapter 15, we will review the evidence that Native Americans are treated more harshly by the criminal justice system, and some studies report that Native Americans are more likely to be sentenced to prison than are whites, even after control for other possible causal variables (e.g., Hall and Simkus, 1975). Hall and Simkus pointed out that this means that Native Americans are more likely to become and be labeled as convicted felons, with resulting stigma. Lemert (1967) has suggested that, if an offender perceives inequalities in the criminal disposition, then he is more likely to accept the imposition of a criminal identity and behave accordingly.

Levy (1988) discussed the problems which arise in preventing suicide among Native Americans which has implications for a social reaction theory of Native American criminal behavior. Research on suicidal behavior among the Shoshoni-Bannock indicated that none of the completed suicides had made prior suicide attempts and that the suicides were found in only eight of the families on the reservation. The majority of the suicides, going back into the nineteenth century, came from only four families. These families had been labeled as deviants and had become scapegoats for the community. Just as one particular family member may be the symptom bearer for a whole family, so in this community these families seemed to bear the symptoms for the whole community. Thus, an effective suicide prevention program would not be one which focused on high risk youth, such as those who had attempted suicide, but rather one which focused on getting to know these few families intimately and working with them to change their status. However, to focus efforts on these families might serve to reinforce their "labelled" status as deviants.

Among the Hopi, Levy found that suicide was not a result of acculturation stress or anomie, but rather concentrated in the children of families who had made deviant marriages, such as when high status female Native Americans took low status male mates who later laid claim to prestigious ceremonial positions. However, to overtly deal with this problem would be to alienate the Hopi. Levy suggested that a successful suicide prevention program needed to appeal to both deviant and non-deviant people in the community, and to avoid identifying with the existing treatment programs or with any theory of the cause of Hopi problems.

Levy and Kunitz (1987) noted that deviant families among the Hopi serve as models for the consequences of deviant behavior and as scapegoats for the community. In one village, a mother and her daughter were both alcohol abusers, and their slovenly appearance and delapidated home were publicly ridiculed. Alcoholism counselors helped the two women overcome their alcohol abuse, whereupon the community increased their abuse, resenting the loss of their "whipping boys." The two women soon became alcohol abusers again.

On the other hand, the Hopi community will occasionally minimize someone's deviant behavior. In a case of mother-son incest, the family refused to bring charges against the son. The family claimed that the sixty-year-old mother was nearly blind and too obese to know what her son was doing to her. In another case, a elderly widower, who raped a five-year-old girl and returned to the community after serving his sentence, had the same status as the other elderly men in the community. To label too many acts and too many people as deviant would destroy social cohesion and threaten the survival. Thus, although the community may disapprove of certain behaviors, they respond officially to only a few instances.

It would be useful if the informal labeling that may take place in Native American communities be studied for its relevance for delinquent and criminal behavior.

Comment

We have seen that social process theories have promise for explaining delinquent and criminal behavior on Native American reservations. However, sound research on the three types of theories has not yet been conducted. Furthermore, these theories may have little applicability to criminal behavior of Native Americans living off the reservations. Indeed, we have very little information on the normal and criminal behavior of Native Americans living off the reservations with which to presently evaluate the usefulness of any of the theories of crime for explaining their criminal behavior.

REFERENCES

Akers, R. L. *Deviant behavior.* Belmont, CA: Wadsworth, 1985.

Bandura, A. *Social learning theory.* Englewood Cliffs, NJ: Prentice-Hall, 1977.

Becker, H. *Outsiders.* New York: Macmillan, 1963.

Hall, E., & Simkus, A. Inequality in the type of sentences received by Native Americans and whites. *Criminology,* 1975, *13,* 199-222.

Hirschi, T. *Causes of delinquency.* Berkeley, CA: University of California, 1969.

Lemert, E. *Human deviance, social problems, and social control.* Englewood Cliffs, NJ: Prentice-Hall, 1967.

Levy, J. E. The effects of labeling on health behavior and treatment programs among North American Indians. *American Indian & Alaska Native Mental Health Research,* 1988, 1, monograph *1,* 211-231.

Levy, J. E., & Kunitz, S. J. A suicide prevention program for Hopi youth. *Social Science & Medicine,* 1987, *25,* 931-940.

Matza, D. *Delinquency and drift.* New York: Wiley, 1964.

Reckless, W. *The crime problem.* New York: Appleton-Century-Crofts, 1967.

Robbins, S. P. Anglo concepts and Indian reality. *Social Casework,* 1984, *65,* 235-241.

Robbins, S. P. Commitment, belief and Native American delinquency. *Human Organization,* 1985, *44,* 57-62.

Schur, E. *Radical nonintervention.* Englewood Cliffs, NJ: Prentice-Hall, 1973.

Sutherland, E. H. *Principles of criminology.* Philadelphia: Lippincott, 1947.

Sutherland, E. H., & Cressey, D. *Criminology.* Philadelphia: Lippincott, 1966.

Sykes, G., & Matza, D. Techniques of neutralization. *American Sociological Review,* 1957, *22,* 664-670.

Winfree, L. T., Griffiths, C. T., & Sellers, C. S. Social learning theory, drug use, and American Indian youths. *Justice Quarterly,* 1989, *6,* 395-416.

Part 4

THE CRIMINAL JUSTICE SYSTEM

Chapter 12

NATIVE AMERICAN POLICING

Prior to 1869, the United States military provided policing for all American tribal reservations. In 1869, the agent for the Iowa and Sac-Fox tribes in Nebraska created the first Native American police force, and this was followed in 1872 by the creation of a Navajo police force.[1] A Native American police force was set up in 1874 at the San Carlos (AZ) Apache reservation to police Native Americans and non-Native Americans. This police force arrested Geronimo and his followers in 1877 without a shot being fired. Recognizing their usefulness, Congress began appropriating funds for Native American police forces in 1879. Much of the effort of these police forces in the late 1800s and early 1900s was directed toward liquor suppression. During Prohibition in 1920s, the number of Native American police officers declined, and the numbers declined still during World War Two.

The 1950s witnessed a trend toward tribal criminal justice autonomy as several tribes, such as the Navajo, improved their criminal justice systems. The Omnibus Crime Control and Safe Streets Act of 1968 funnelled several million dollars into Native American criminal justice agencies. The Indian Civil Rights Act, also in 1968, mandated further improvements in Native American criminal justice procedures, including holding tribal courts to due process standards and permitting defendants to have legal counsel present in court.

Peak (1994) reported that there were currently 623 federal Native American law enforcement personnel—124 special agents (criminal investigators), 336 police officers, 59 resource officers, and 104 guards in detention centers. In addition, there were 1636 nonfederal personnel, that is, tribal officers working independently but supported by the Bureau of Indian Affairs. The 1994 budget of the Bureau of Indian

---

1. This section is based on Wachtel (1980, 1981) and Peak (1994).

Affairs for these services was $84 million, and $80 million for 1998 (Anon, 1998).

Tribal policing has resulted in several problems. Tribal police departments are sometimes plagued by nepotism, poor training, low pay, high turnover and poor equipment. The Native Americans often view the tribal police as simply agents of the white oppressors, and tribal council members often campaign on anti-police platforms, further eroding the status of the police officers.

Nash (1984) noted that in 1982, there were 182 Native American reservations with law enforcement programs in 24 states. There were 1,509 full-time Native American law enforcement personnel, providing services to a Native American population of 475,413 spread over 106,000 square miles. They recorded 187,574 criminal complaints, investigated 103,605 arrests or citations, gave 46,518 traffic warnings, and provided 587,310 nonenforcement services. The average case load per officer was 765.

The Navajo Police Force

The Navajo police force, established in 1872, was disbanded only a few years later, and policing was taken over by the military and the Bureau of Indian Affairs until 1958, when the tribe created its own police department. As of 1980, the department had 473 full-time employees, including 338 sworn police officers, with a budget of $9 million. The department polices 160,000 people spread over 25,000 square miles. Serious offenses are handled by outside agencies. The Bureau of Indian Affairs handles all cases of rape, arson and larceny, and robbery, burglary and welfare fraud over $2,000 and all crimes committed by non-Native Americans.[2]

The Division of Public Safety runs the police department, a planning section and an internal affairs section. The police department is run by an officer with rank of Lieutenant Colonel. It has two field units and an administrative unit, each run by an officer with the rank of major. There are six districts, each run by a captain who must supervise the uniformed patrol, criminal investigation unit, jail management and support services for the district.

---

2. The United States Supreme Court in *Oliphant v. Squamish* [(1977). 431 U.S. 964] held that tribal courts may not try non-Native Americans (Barsh and Henderson, 1979).

The Navajo reservation lies in three states (Arizona, New Mexico and Utah), and nine counties in these states. Thus, the police department must coordinate with many different state and local agencies and policies. Training for the Navajo police officer involves a 20-week residential basic course. The officers must learn about the laws in all three states and nine counties. In addition, because of the rugged terrain, officers must learn to repel from cliffs, skin dive, ride horses, and conduct search-and-rescue missions. In addition to normal police duties, they must also learn how to handle uniquely Navajo problems such as accusations of witchcraft and crowd control at ceremonies such as the Squaw Dance.

The Navajo police officer has great discretionary power, and this, as well as other duties and functions, is strongly affected by the fact that he is a local Navajo, policing the district from which he came, so that he knows everyone is his district and is well known to the citizens in his district.

However, the Navajo police officer has, to some extent, weakened in his adherence to traditional Navajo values. Wachtel (1981) administered a questionnaire to a sample of the police officers and found that over 90 percent had been born and raised on the reservation and that two-thirds had been raised by both parents. A quarter were military veterans, and three-quarters were Christians. They tended to be young, inexperienced and unmarried.

The vast majority of Navajo police officers felt that Navajo officers should not wear their hair in the traditional manner (long, tied up in a bun for formal occasions), did not feel that they should give fellow Navajos a break, and thought that intoxicated Navajos gave the tribe a bad reputation. Thus, Wachtel concluded that the Navajo police officers rejected some Navajo traditions. On the other hand, the majority of the officers felt that only Navajos should be permitted to become police officers on the reservation.

Feinman (1986) noted several problems faced by the Navajo police officers. As noted above, Navajo police officers must be cognizant of federal, state and local laws as well as Navajo Nation laws. There is some resentment toward the federal law enforcement agencies and officers. The Navajo claim that the federal authorities do not prosecute many of the serious crimes that fall within federal jurisdiction. In 1982 to 1983, only 18 convictions were handed down for 802 felonies, and the Navajo argue that federal authorities ignore their responsibilities and duties if the victim in a Native American.

There are other problems for the Navajo police officer. Learning the laws of all the different jurisdictions makes training more burdensome for the Navajo police officer. Having to handle over cases to local, state and federal authorities when required frustrates and insults Navajo police officers by implying that they would not be able to handle the crime if non-Native Americans are involved or if the crime is a felony. The Anglo criminal justice system is based on customs and mores which are not congruent with Navajo culture–apprehension and punishment rather than mediation, consensus and restitution.

Furthermore, the Navajo police are viewed with distrust and suspicion by other Navajos–they are seen as tools of the Anglo oppressors, enforcing the laws and customs of these oppressors. Some members of the American Indian Movement (AIM) have openly expressed this viewpoint (Young, 1990). This, of course, is a problem faced by police officers who belong to any cultural group. For example, African American police officers face this problem with African Americans in the community.[3]

Policing on the Navajo reservation is made difficult also by the fact that half of the Navajo population is 18-years-old or younger, by the high rates of alcohol abuse[4] and by the problems facing all police officers in America, such as low pay, few opportunities for promotion, and little respect from the community. In addition, police work on the reservation is lonely–because of the size of the reservation, the responsibilities average out to about one Navajo police officer for every 1,200 people and 135 square miles of territory.

Wachtel (1983) reported a study of the use of discretion by Navajo police officers, a study unfortunately marred by severe errors in its write-up. Wachtel claimed to have measured discretion through personal observation of the police officers in patrol cars and in the booking area. However, he gives no account of how discretion was measured and for which deviant behaviors. He explored twelve predictors of the use of discretion, but reports data in his tables on only eleven. He claims that four predictors were significant as predictors, but notes only three in this tables. Finally, the focus of his study was on traditional values in the police officers as predictors of discretion, and he

---

3. I once had a student in my college class in the 1960s who was a police officer fighting with dissident students on a nearby university campus during the campus disturbances by day, while becoming a student himself at night and hiding his occupation from his fellow students.

4. The prohibition of the sale of alcohol on the reservation makes bootlegging common, but the Navajo police officer receives little cooperation from the community in policing this.

concluded both "the traditionality measures are of no significance in the analysis" and "the findings show a connection between the use of discretion by the police officer and his traditionality" (Wachtel, 1983, p. 60), a seeming contradiction.

What can we conclude from Wachtel's study? Police officers who were Christian, younger, with military experience and whose mothers were born off the reservation were less likely to use discretion. Wachtel argues that these variables reflect less traditionality. On the other hand, more direct measures of traditionality, including knowing your clan name, speaking the tribal language and agreeing with traditional values did not predict the use of discretion. (In addition, the father's birthplace, years of police experience and education did not predict the use of discretion.)

Thus, perhaps the less traditional Navajo police officers were less likely to use discretion in their work, but we need a much better study on this issue before we can conclude that this conclusion is reliable.

Policing in Alaska

Rural Alaska is large, with 100,000 people living in the over 200 villages spread over the 350 million acres, including Eskimos, Aleuts and Native Americans. Although the law enforcement agencies occasionally employ Natives as officers, the first systematic attempt to recruit Native officers was initiated in the 1960s when they were trained as village police officers (VPOs), supervised by the Alaska State Troopers. The program was plagued by many problems (Marenin and Copus, 1991; Marenin, 1992). Funding was a problem, especially after the start-up funding from the Law Enforcement Assistance Administration dried up. Turnover rates were large, probably as a result of the difficulties of the job and the low salaries. The training provided for the officers did not appear to be sufficient, the officers themselves did not perform their jobs well, and the goals of the program were never made clear.

Accordingly, in the 1980s, a new program was initiated—the Village Public Safety Officer (VPSO). This program was designed to be more under the control of the local village councils, although the Alaska State Troopers supervised the officers as before. Similar problems were found in this new program, although perhaps less so (Marenin and Copus, 1991), but the program seems to have had a beneficial impact on violence and alcohol abuse in some villages. However, Marenin and Copus have noted that no adequate evaluation of the program had been made at the time of their report.[5]

Canada

In Canada, Griffiths (1988) noted that there is much hostility between Native Canadians and whites. Most policing of Native Canadians is by non-Natives and even Native Canadian-oriented programs are mostly controlled by non-Natives. Skoog et al. (1980) surveyed Native Canadians and whites in Manitoba and found that, although the overall view of the police was positive, whites were more positive than Native Canadians, regardless of age, sex or urban/rural location. For example, only 68 percent of the Native Canadians felt that the police provided adequate protection for themselves and their families versus 86 percent of whites.

Griffiths (1988) noted that the program using Native Canadian police officers run by the Royal Canadian Mounted Police has little Native community input, a lack of a clear role for the Native Canadian police officers, and a reluctance of the part of Native Canadians to join the force. The program run by Ontario has a much better image. Recently, some Native Canadian-run police forces have appeared (in Quebec and Manitoba, for example), and these have been viewed quite positively by the communities they serve.

Police officers are reluctant or slow to respond to Native Canadian calls for assistance and, when they do get involved, tend to assert there authority and are enforcement-oriented. Many police officers have little knowledge about Native Canadians, especially younger officers. Older, experienced officers are viewed more positively, however.

Griffiths noted that no published evaluations on these programs have appeared, either on the reserves or in the urban areas to which Native Canadians have migrated.

---

5. Griffiths and Yerbury (1984) noted similar problems with a program to establish a Native Special Constable Program in Canada – conflict between the police officers and the communities, failure of the Royal Canadian Mounted Police to define the role of the Special Constables clearly, shorter training, low pay, fewer opportunities for promotion, an ambiguous role for the Special Constables, and lack of Native input into the program.

Coordination Between Agencies

The potential conflicts between tribal and government agencies led the International Association of Chiefs of Police to set up a committee to explore cooperative relationships for these groups (Nash, 1984). Nash illustrated the process of obtaining cooperation with the Umatilla Indian Reservation in Umatilla County, Oregon. In 1953, Public Law 280[6] ended federal and tribal law enforcement operations on the reservation and turned policing over to Umatilla County Sheriff's Department and the Oregon State Police. In 1975, the Umatilla tribe began to discuss how they might change back to the tribal-federal structure, setting up their own police force and criminal court.

Meetings were arranged involving all tribal, local, state and federal agencies involved. With the cooperation of everyone, the governor of Oregon signed an executive order in 1980 offering the state's authority over the reservation back to the federal government. The offer was accepted. The new Umatilla tribal police department started with nine sworn officers plus dispatchers and office staff. The tribal police have commissions in the sheriff's department and federal commissions from the Bureau of Indian Affairs; the county sheriff's staff and the local state police personnel have commissions from the tribal police department. Thus, any officer can take action in any situation. However, there is a gentlemen's agreement which governs the patrol responsibilities, with the tribal police patrolling and handling cases on the reservation. If a situation on the reservation involves a state violation, the tribal police act as state police officers. The tribe has contracted with the county sheriff's department for detention at the county jail and juvenile detention center.

Barker and Mullen (1993) noted that cross-deputization between Native American and local police departments is not a uniform policy across the United States and, although there are obvious advantages, there may also be problems. There are fears among Native American communities that it weakens their sovereignty, local police departments sometimes feel that the Native American police officers are not trained well, and Native American residents fear victimization at the hands of the local police officers.

---

6. This law mandated six states to assume exclusive criminal jurisdiction over crimes committed by Native Americans on reservations and permitted other states to do so if they wished.

Barker and Mullen surveyed 104 tribal police departments but received completed surveys from only 31. Of these, 26 (84%) had some agreement with local police departments in force. They indicated that such agreements developed when Native American and local agencies had good relations and when there were statewide guidelines for such agreements (as in New Mexico). The size of the Native American community, the existence of a functional 911 system, the presence of a tribal jail, the number of Native American police officers and the percentage of police officers who were Native Americans did not predict the presence of an agreement.

Willis et al. (1992) provided an example of the possible deleterious consequences of multiagency involvement in criminal justice when there is no cooperation and coordination between the agencies.

A fourteen-year-old girl was reported to the school counselor because of alleged sexual abuse by her natural father, with whom she lived. The school counselor contacted the Indian Child Welfare worker, who had no previous experience or training in sexual abuse interventions. The county human services department declined to become involved due to lack of jurisdiction. The FBI was contacted, who stated that they could not respond immediately but recommended that the counselor proceed with the investigation. The tribal/BIA police were contacted but refused to assist due to lack of training in the area. The ICW worker made an appointment for a medical examination, interviewed the girl on three separate occasions, and submitted an investigative report to the FBI. When the FBI received the report and read it, they declined to prosecute due to the inadequate evidence in the report.

The tribal court prosecutor was contacted but declined to prosecute due to the lack of authority over a major crime. The ICW worker again contacted the FBI and asked for assistance. The FBI responded by going out and interviewing the girl, contacting the alleged perpetrator, and proceeding with their own investigation.

Approximately five weeks later, the FBI declined to prosecute, stating that the initial investigation by the ICW had been done so poorly that the evidence could not be used in the federal court system. The case never went to court. (Willis et al., 1992, p. 281.)

Since the FBI acknowledged eventually that it was their task to investigate a major crime, they should be held responsible for the failure to obtain adequate evidence. In addition, the refusal of the tribal police/BIA to assist the ICW worker also makes them responsible. The personnel of both of these agencies should both have been severely disciplined, but it is very unlikely that any personnel were punished.

Comment

Most of this research and commentary has focused on policing on Native American reservations, and very little attention has been given to policing Native Americans in the general community. On the reservations, some programs have been implemented which have promise, including the developing police force on the Navajo reservation and the cooperative programs involving the Umatilla tribe.

REFERENCES

Anon. Signs of hope for Indian country policing. *Law Enforcement News*, 1998, *24*(488), 17.

Barker, M. L., & Mullen, K. Cross-deputization in Indian country. *Police Studies*, 1993, *16*, 157-166.

Barsh, R. L., & Henderson, J. Y. The betrayal. *Minnesota Law Review*, 1979, *63*, 609-640.

Feinman, C. Police problems on the Navajo reservation. *Police Studies*, 1986, *9*, 194-198.

Griffiths, C. T. Native Indians and the police. *Police Studies*, 1988, *11*, 155-160.

Griffiths, C. T., & Yerbury, J. C. Natives and criminal justice policy. *Canadian Journal of Criminology*, 1984, *26*, 147-160.

Marenin, O. Policing the last frontier. *Policing & Society*, 1992, *2*, 273-291.

Marenin, O., & Copus, G. Policing rural Alaska. *American Journal of Police*, 1991, *10*(4), 1-26.

Nash, D. R. Tribal law enforcement. *Police Chief*, 1984, *51*(4), 26-28.

Peak, K. Policing and crime in Indian country. *Journal of Contemporary Criminal Justice*, 1994, *10*, 79-94.

Skoog, D., Roberts, L. W., & Boldt, E. D. Native attitudes toward the police. *Canadian Journal of Criminology*, 1980, *22*, 354-359.

Wachtel, D. A historical look at BIA police on the reservations. *American Indian Quarterly*, 1980, *6*(5), 13-18.

Wachtel, D. The Navajo police officer. *Quarterly Journal of Ideology*, 1981, *11*(4), 71-82.

Wachtel, D. The effects of traditionalism on the Navajo police officer. *Police Studies*, 1983, *6*(3), 57-62.

Willis, D. J., Dobrec, A., & Snipes, D. S. B. Treating American Indian victims of abuse and neglect. In L. A. Vargas & J. D. Koss-Chioino (Eds.), *Working with culture*, pp. 276-299. San Francisco: Jossey-Bass, 1992.

Young, T. J. Native American crime and criminal justice require criminologists' attention. *Journal of Criminal Justice Education*, 1990, *1*, 111-116.

Chapter 13

THE LAW AND THE COURTS

This book is not intended to explore the complex legal issues and decision involving Native Americans. However, it is worth noting a few unique features of the law as it involves Native Americans.

A Brief Summary of Early Events[1]

Although the official policy in the later 1600s was to purchase land from Native Americans tribes, they were also forced to move westwards by force. President George Washington appointed his Secretary of War, Henry Knox, to administer the government's Native American policy, and Knox sought congressional protection for Native Americans through the passage of laws which prevented such acts as settling on Native American lands and driving livestock through their lands. In 1799, the sale of distribution of alcohol to Native Americans was prohibited.

In 1817, the General Crimes Act provided that crimes committed on Native American lands would be adjudicated by state and federal courts in the same manner as elsewhere in the United States.

Under President Andrew Jackson, the federal government returned to a policy of forced displacement of the Native Americans toward the West, a policy formalized by the Indian Removal Act in 1830. In the 1850s, 174 million acres of land were acquired from Native Americans by treaty, while in the 1860s California began setting up Native American reservations in the midst of non-Native American land.

Native Americans were granted citizenship and voting rights in 1924, although some states tried to circumvent this. For example,

---

1. This section is based on Peak (1994) and Shattuck and Norgren (1979).

Arizona continued to bar Native Americans from voting, while Idaho denied the right to "Indians not taxed." It was not until 1976 that the United States Supreme Court eliminated these impediments.

The reservation system makes for great complications. The American Constitution can often come into conflict with tribal values. For example, the United States Supreme Court in 1977 upheld a tribal rule that only children of Pueblo fathers could be members of the tribe, despite the sex discrimination involved in this tribal rule.

Since Native Americans have a special legal relationship with the American government, the federal government can prevent state jurisdictional encroachments. On the other hand, the federal government can also intervene and undermine tribal authority. In addition, Congress can intervene in Native American affairs, such as abrogating treaty obligations and extinguishing Native title to lands.

Unlike some other minority groups, until recently Native Americans did not have a public legal interest organization. Thus, Native American litigation was less coordinated and programmatic in challenging the dominant system. Legal rights vary from tribe to tribe, and the planning of a common strategy has been more difficult. The establishment of the Native American Rights Fund in the 1970s has improved this situation to some extent, as the organization has formulated policies and strategies relevant to tribal existence and resources, protection of treaty-guaranteed lands, social benefits and cultural autonomy.

Young et al. (1987) commented on what they called "international" issues since some Native American tribes consider themselves to be separate national powers.

(1) Some tribes are trying to recover lands that were taken from them. For example, the Lakotas have tried to recover the Black Hills of South Dakota.

(2) Some tribes are fighting over water rights. For example, the Soboba tribe has fought to recover rights for its water which was diverted to the Los Angeles Metropolitan Water District.

(3) Problems arise between tribes. For example, The 1974 Relocation Act removed over 10,000 Navajos from an area claimed by the Hopi, resulting in conflict between the two tribes.

(4) Some of tribes with oil reserves on their land have tried to deal directly with OPEC, the international oil cartel.

The Navajo Tribal Court System

Tso (1989) noted that prior to conquest by whites, the Navajo had several procedures for resolving problems. Settling disputes via mediation, compensation of victims and diversion were common practices, ideas which Anglos have only recently "discovered" and introduced. In addition, it has been recognized that the Navajo had a system of *customary law*, which is now recognized to be equivalent to *common law* and which the Navajo Nation Supreme Court is developing through case decisions.

Navajo courts were first established in 1882, dominated at first by white agents appointed by the federal government, then after 1935 by a white law enforcement officer from the Bureau of Indian Affairs, and from 1951 to 1959 by a Navajo elected by popular vote. In 1959, the Navajo tribal council created a judicial branch, with six judges, each in charge of one trial court, and a chief justice appointed by the chairman of the Navajo tribe, approved by the tribal council and trained by the council's legal staff (Shepardson, 1965).

The Navajo tribal code was based on the administrative law of the federal code, but modified by decisions of the tribal council.[2] Candidates for judges are screened for knowledge of English and Navajo, intelligence test scores and personal character. After two years probation, they are tenured. The court are run formally, modeled on courts in general in the United States. However, there are differences. Lawyers may not represent clients in the tribal courts, there is no verbatim record made of the proceedings, appeals are not based on errors but involve instead a re-hearing of the case, and the customary law of the Navajos may be administered as well as codified law.

In 1960, the police and courts handled 10,699 actions, of which 7,359 were for disorderly conduct and 1,658 for liquor violations. About 20 percent of the cases are civil complaints brought by Navajos.

In the old, traditional system for handling disputes, the people involved and their families took the initiative, called all interested parties together, chose mediators and tired to settle the matter. Some Navajos still follow this procedure, while others use the tribal judge as the mediator. Sanctions, when imposed, are enforced by "nagging" or "shaming" the guilty party.

---

2. For a description of the operation of the Navajo tribal court system, see Tso (1989).

The formal proceedings of the Navajo court are made difficult by language problems (since the legal code is in English), by the cost involved and by the distances people have to travel to the courts. Judges also have to decide when to apply the legal code and when to apply customary law.

Many of the acts of the Navajo police and courts are simply impositions of law devised by the federal government by force—such as outlawing peyote, polygyny and union organizing. Thus, many of the laws are considered unjust and are evaded or resisted. If the community thinks that a court decision was wrong, they may revert to traditional processes. Shepardson described the case of a Navajo who was found not guilty of murder because it was self-defense, but was still forced by the community to pay compensation to the dead man's family.

Civil actions include those in which the judge is used as a mediator as in the traditional get-togethers, where judges administer customary law (as in probate cases),[3] for modern formalities such as getting marriages validated, divorces recorded, estates probated, and suits for non-support of dependent children, and for taking advantage of federal law, such as a spouse who wants to share an inheritance which would formerly be passed down the matrilineal line.

Tribal courts have been plagued by problems of many kinds. Brakel (1976) noted that the facilities are often quite poor, and there is a lack of clerical and technical support. The judges and prosecutors sometimes have no legal training. Defendants plead guilty far too often and frequently have no lawyer representing them. Appeals are also rare.[4]

Restorative Justice

The ways in which the Navajo tribal courts have introduced traditional custom into their processes falls under the rubric of *restorative justice* (Galaway and Hudson, 1996). In this view, crime is viewed as a conflict between people which harms all involved as well as the community. The aim is to create peace by reconciling the parties involved and repairing the injuries, with active participation by victims and offenders and the whole community.

---

3. For example, medicine bags traditionally are given to those most skilled in using them rather than to direct descendants, a custom which sometimes causes friction.

4. For a good review of the system see Deloria and Lytle (1983).

The peacemaking system introduced into the Navajo court system using mediators falls into this type of system (Yazzie and Zion, 1996), and examples can be found in Native Canadian communities also, such as "sentencing circles" (Stuart, 1996) and Youth Justice Committees (Nielsen, 1996).

The Provision of Legal Services for Urban Native Americans

Chadwick et al. (1976) noted that in 1970, almost half of all Native Americans lived in urban areas. Many of these are newcomers to city life, and they must learn how to conform to urban legal norms. They are often taken advantage of by merchants, landlords and employers, and they often have little awareness of legal and social services available to them. Even if they are aware of these services, they may distrust them because they are staffed by members of other ethnic groups, and they may be put off by the attitudes and behaviors of the non-Native American staff at these agencies who may have very little understanding of the cultural norms of Native Americans or the problems they face.

In Seattle, Washington, there are many services available for Native Americans, often with no charge, at the local, state and federal level. To explore this, Chadwick surveyed one hundred Native Americans in Seattle, using Native American interviewers, and a sample of whites. The Native Americans reported a rate of arrest in Seattle of 24 per 100 compared to 4 for the whites. The whites reported much more consumer fraud than the Native Americans, such as being sold faulty goods (32% versus 19%), in all areas except being charged high interest rates (6 percent versus 5 percent). However, more Native Americans had civil actions initiated against them than the whites, such as receiving abusive letters from creditors (22% versus 13%).

Of course, the Native Americans were less educated and poorer than the whites in the sample. However, the number of reported legal problems was not associated with education, poverty or the length of time residing in the city.

A greater percentage of the Native Americans than whites had utilized the legal services available, such as the Office of Economic Opportunity's legal services (8% versus 2%). However, only ten percent of Native Americans arrested had been represented by a lawyer, and fewer Native Americans were aware of the services available. For example, only 39 percent of the Native Americans knew of the Lawyer's Referral Office as compared to 70 percent of the whites. One-fifth of the Native Americans thought that the free services "cost too much!" Many Native Americans did not know what a lawyer was, and others felt that the services were primarily for African Americans.

In the light of their findings, Chadwick and his colleagues urged an educational and informational campaign to inform Native Americans of what services existed, to emphasize that the services are free and to ensure that the staff are sensitive to Native American needs and styles. In addition, extensive outreach programs should be initiated by the relevant agencies to reach the Native American community, such as placing workers in police stations, in jails and prisons and in skid row sections of cities.

Halverson (1972), a lawyer of Native American descent, visited various Native American centers in Seattle on a regular weekly basis for five weeks to determine the need for legal counseling. Halverson concluded that Native Americans have a profound distrust of governmental agencies. They have a greater involvement with the law than whites, but also far less knowledge of the criminal justice system. For example, many do know about the simple Miranda warnings, and those who know their rights are afraid to exercise them.

Halverson interviewed thirty clients, only one of whom had contacted a government agency before seeing Halverson. Some had had legal problems for two years, but Halverson was the first lawyer they had consulted. Halverson suggested that having Native Americans on the staff was critical for helping Native Americans for it was unlikely that Native Americans would approach non-Natives in intimidating settings.

Comment

The issues involved differ considerably for Native Americans who live on reservations than for Native Americans living in the general community. The functioning of the tribal courts has not been studied much at all in order to monitor what happens and what factors determine outcomes. For Native Americans living in the general community, again only one study has explored the legal problem they face dealing with the American criminal justice system, and this was only in urban areas. Clearly, the issues involved in these topics are urgently in need of further study.

Reform Of The Criminal Justice System

Incidentally, Mann (1993) noted that Native Americans tried off the reservation are rarely tried by juries with any Native American members and so are not tried by their "peers." Not only do they often lack defense counsel, there are rarely any Native American defense counselors available to defend them and rarely, if ever, any Native American judges.

REFERENCES

Brakel, S. J. American Indian tribal courts. *American Bar Association Journal,* 1976, *62,* 1002-1006.

Chadwick, B. A., Stauss, J., Bahr, H. M., & Halverson, L. K. Confrontation with the law. *Phylon,* 1976, *37*(2), 163-171.

Deloria, V., & Lytle, C. M. *American Indians, American justice.* Austin, TX: University of Texas, 1983.

Galaway, B., & Hudson, J. (Eds.). *Restorative justice.* Monsey, NY: Criminal Justice Press, 1996.

Halverson, L. K. Report on legal services to the Indians. In H. M. Bahr, B. A. Chadwick & R. C. Day (Eds.), *Native Americans today,* pp. 338-344. New York: Harper & Row, 1972.

Mann, C. R. *Unequal justice.* Indianapolis, IN: University of Indiana, 1993.

Nielsen, M. O. A comparison of developmental ideologies. In B. Galaway & J. Hudson (Eds.), *Restorative justice,* pp. 207-223. Monsey, NY: Criminal Justice Press, 1996.

Peak, K. Policing and crime in Indian country. *Journal of Contemporary Criminal Justice,* 1994, *10,* 79-94.

Shattuck, P. T., & Norgren, J. Political use of the legal process by black and American Indian minorities. *Howard Law Journal,* 1979, *22,* 1-26.

Shepardson, M. Problems of the Navajo Tribal Courts in transition. *Human Organization,* 1965, *24,* 250-253.

Stuart, B. Circle sentencing. In B. Galaway & J. Hudson (Eds.), *Restorative justice,* pp. 194-206. Monsey, NY: Criminal Justice Press, 1996.

Tso, T. The process of decision making in tribal courts. *Arizona Law Review,* 1989, *31,* 225-235.

Yazzie, R., & Zion, J. W. Navajo restorative justice. In B. Galaway & J. Hudson (Eds.), *Restorative justice*, pp. 157-173. Monsey, NY: Criminal Justice Press, 1996.

Young, T. J., LaPlante, C., & Robbins, W. Indians before the law. *Quarterly Journal of Ideology*, 1987, *11*(4), 59-70.

Chapter 14

PRISONS AND PROBATION

It is commonly noted in scholarly reports that Native Americans are overrepresented in American prisons. Some typical data, in this case from Flowers (1990) for 1983, are presented in Table 14.1. It can be seen that Native Americans were incarcerated in federal and state prisons at a higher rate than all ethnic groups except African Americans and Hispanic Americans.

Who's in Prison?

Grobsmith (1994) interviewed some of the Native American prisoners in the Nebraska system. She found a pattern of early childhood involvement with alcohol and drugs, family disintegration, minor delinquent acts, leading to criminal convictions. Inhalant use was common at an early age, and users came from homes where alcohol abuse and child abuse and neglect were common. Inhalants cause brain damage (as well as other physiological problems such as kidney dysfunction) and may facilitate the appearance of violent behavior. Gaining access to inhalants often involves minor delinquencies, such as petty theft and vandalism.

The inmates interviewed by Grobsmith typically had their first arrest at age 14 and averaged 19 arrests prior to incarceration. The lifetime number of arrests was 29, and the inmates had served time in jails or prisons about 12 times. About a quarter had relatives who had been arrested. Most had alcoholic parents, and a quarter had suffered abuse at the hands of their parents.

The problem with these data from Grobsmith, of course, is that she did not compare the lives of these Native American inmates with inmates from other ethnic groups, nor with noncriminal Native

Americans. Thus, it is impossible to draw sound implications from her data.

Native Americans could not typically afford to hire private lawyers. Plea bargaining was the rule, with three-quarters pleading guilty to lesser or fewer charges. The most common offenses were, in order, burglary, theft, first-degree sexual assault, and robbery. Most of the crimes, including the sexual assaults, were carried out while intoxicated, and all of Grobsmith's sample claimed to be chemically addicted.

Alcohol and drugs were readily available in prison, and forty percent of the Native American inmates admitted to using them while in prison. There were treatment programs for inmates who were alcohol and drug abusers, but Native Americans tended to dislike the programs run by non-Natives. The Native American inmates preferred to avoid the therapy programs (which are mandatory if a sexual offender wishes to be paroled early) and to serve out their time without seeking parole, even if the programs were oriented toward Native Americans. The Native American inmates preferred the traditional techniques for treating alcohol abuse, such as the sweat lodges.

The Native American inmates accepted supervision and restriction while in prison, but resented it when on parole. Of 42 Native American inmates studied by Grobsmith, only 26 chose parole, with 16 choosing to serve their complete sentence. Seventeen of the 26 paroled were rearrested for parole violations or new crimes, including 70 percent of those paroled into inpatient treatment programs.

In Minnesota in the early 1970s, Benjamin and Kim (1980) compared white and Native American prisoners. They found that the Native Americans were more often from urban areas, less often from "normal" family groupings (that is, they were more often not married, with no dependents and not living with parents or spouse), less educated, more often with alcohol problems but less often with drug problems, had more total correctional records but no more prior felony convictions.[1]

Canada

Lane et al. (1978) surveyed 316 Native Canadian inmates in penitentiaries across Canada in 1977. About half were aged 25 or younger;

---

1. The groups did not differ in skill level, unemployment or mental and physical problems

64 percent had been convicted of offenses against person (primarily robbery with violence) and 36 percent with crimes against property (primarily breaking and entering). Forty-five percent were in maximum security institutions and 41 percent in medium security institutions. Fifty-four percent of the offenses occurred in urban areas, 30 percent in rural areas and 16 percent on reservations. Ninety percent of the offenders were under the influence of alcohol, drugs or both at the time of the offense. Half of the inmates had spent time on skid row.

Sixty-eight percent had been raised in rural areas, about half in racially mixed areas. Half had relatives who had been in prison while they were growing up, and two-thirds had friends who had been in prison. Seventy-nine percent had been in foster homes or institutions for some period before the age of sixteen, and sixty-three percent had left home before the age of 16.

LaPrairie (1984) reviewed a number of unpublished reports on Native Canadian women in prison. She noted that Native Canadian women constituted a greater proportion of female inmates in federal and provincial prisons than their proportion in the population. In Ontario, 37 percent of the Native Canadian female prisoners in 1982 were twenty years of age or less, 52 percent had been arrested between the ages of 14 to 17, and 40 percent had been arrested fifteen times or more. Native Canadian females arrested were less likely to be released on bail than whites and less often fined, probably because of the greater likelihood that they were destitute.[2] Alcohol played a role in a greater proportion of the crimes of Native Canadian women than of whites. In the federal prisons, Native Canadian females were more often serving time for violent crimes and less often for property crimes.

Native American Detention Centers

In 1988, there were a total of 3,316 local jails in the United States with a population of 343,569 (Duclos et al., 1994). For the 304 federal Native American reservations, 224 provided some law enforcement, but they had only 72 detention facilities. These were primarily small buildings, built in the 1960s and 1970s, designed as maximum securi-

2. In Canada, Native American women who marry white men cease to be "Indian," thereby having to leave the reservation, dispose of all property they own and forfeiting inheritance rights. These consequences can be devastating.

ty institutions. More than 95 percent of the inmates of these facilities were there because of alcoholism or alcohol-related offenses, typically repeat offenders. The design of the institutions did not lend itself to rehabilitation programs, and they were usually understaffed.

As we noted in Chapter 13, many reservations have quasi-sovereign status with their own laws and government. The Omaha Nation, with 2,500 members spread over 54,000 acres in northeast Nebraska, has a measure of self-determination, but limited resources for total self-suffi- ciency. The tribal courts are organized like typical courts, with judges, prosecutors, juries, etc., and, until recently, could impose a maximum sentence of six months in jail and a $500 fine. This was raised in 1987 to one year in jail and a $1,000 fine (Martin, 1988). The reservation opened a new jail in 1987 constructed for the tribe by the Bureau of Indian Affairs. It is a 32-bed facility, managed by four dispatchers/jail officers and in the late 1980s held an average of fifteen inmates a day.

Martin (1988) noted several major problems with the new jail. It has serious design deficiencies, and the tribe does not have enough resources to operate it properly. With respect to design: (1) the cells could not be observed from a central staff post; (2) the detoxification and safety cells were isolated from the rest of the facility and so diffi- cult to monitor; (3) the housing units had no showers or dayrooms, necessitating prisoners being taken to a centralized shower area with little privacy; (4) outer doors were of solid steel, with no windows, threatening the safety of officers when entering those areas; (5) the cor- ridors had several blind corners; (6) circulation paths for some activi- ties led prisoners of one classification through areas for prisoners of other classifications; (7) the central dining facility had an unlocked door to the outside; and (8) gun cabinets were limited and unlocked.

There were separate sections for female and juvenile inmates, but there were not enough staff to use these facilities. The National Institute of Corrections, which was called in for advice, estimated that a staff of 29 was required to run the facility, whereas the tribe had a staff of four available. Since Congress authorizes funds for each tribe separately, the tribe would have to lobby Congress for increases in funding for the jail.

Martin noted that the Bureau of Indian Affairs was working to cor- rect the problems in this jail, but it is amazing that the bureau would build such a facility without consulting with jail-design experts and with tribal members. Martin's report indicated that the Bureau of Indian Affairs staff involved were incompetent.

Martin noted also that reform of the tribal jail system has been impeded by the lack of law suits brought by prisoners, actions which have led to reforms and improvements in other jail systems.

Martin noted that there are approximately 233 recognized tribes in America, and the Bureau of Indian Affairs has some responsibility for 177 of these tribes, located in 27 states. For law enforcement, the bureau has 141 jails. In 1986, these jails included 43 tribally-owned and operated jails, 26 bureau-owned and operated jails, 20 jails operated by the tribes under contract with the bureau, 39 local county jails under contract with the bureau, and 13 local county jails under contract with the local tribes.

Martin noted that, at the time of his article, the Bureau of Indian Affairs was looking for new design concepts to improve future tribal jails and to minimize the staff required to run them. It hoped to establish comprehensive standards, set up an inspection unit, upgrade training for jail staff, and set up a management information system to help the bureau keep track of offenders in tribal jails (which would assist the Bureau in making budget requests, among other things).

Juveniles in Detention

Duclos et al. (1994) studied the juveniles in three reservation detention centers. In Location A, the booking rate was 4,426 per 100,000 youths per year. Forty-one percent of the bookings occurred on Saturdays and Sundays and 50 percent between 4 P.M. and midnight (with an additional 25 percent between midnight and 8 A.M.). The average age of the juveniles was 15.2 years, and 21 percent were female. Six percent were charged with offenses against persons, 22 percent with property offenses, 22 percent with disturbing the peace, and 10 percent for being beyond the control of their guardians. Twenty-four percent of the offenses were attributable to substance abuse, and 96 percent of the juveniles were detained for less than 24 hours. Data from the other two locations were similar.

Suicide in Custody

As we have seen, Native Americans who commit crimes against tribal, local government or federal laws, on or off the reservation, can be placed in a variety of facilities operated by the tribes, the Bureau of Indian Affairs, and city, county, state or federal authorities. The majority of inmates in these jails are detained because of alcohol-related offenses.

The profile of the typical jail suicide in America is a young male detained for minor offenses, often alcohol-related (Lester and Danto, 1993), and the typical Native American inmate of reservation jails fits this profile.

Most of the jails are designed as maximum security facilities. Adequate supervision of the cells requires a greater number of staff than is typically available, and only intermittent patrol of the cell blocks takes place. At nights, often only the police dispatcher is available for supervising the inmates of the jail. In such situations, inmate suicidal behavior is likely to be more common. In many jurisdictions, Native American youth are housed with adult prisoners, a practice that has been shown in the United States as a whole to increase the risk of youth suicide (Flaherty, 1983)

Duclos et al. (1994a, 1994b) enumerated the various ways in which Native American jails need to be improved: there are limited historical data with which to compare trends; the jails have rudimentary information systems (for example, they are typically not computerized), and the Bureau of Indian Affairs failed to collect any data from 1986 to 1996; the various agencies are fragmented and often do not cooperate; the documentation about inmates is often inadequate and inaccurate (it is for legal rather than management purposes); much suicidal behavior goes undocumented because of the tolerant attitude of the criminal justice personnel toward the inmates and because of the stigma which may be attached to suicide in the community, and this lack of documentation extends to the warning signs for suicidal behavior; suicide risk assessments are rarely conducted on new inmates; the detention staff lack training in mental health and suicide prevention; the design of the facilities is often poor from the standpoint of suicide prevention; and the jails are grossly understaffed, often with only a dispatcher present.

All in all, detention facilities for Native Americans fail most of the recommendations and standards proposed for preventing inmate suicidal behavior (Lester and Danto, 1993).

The Data

Duclos et al. (1994) surveyed the four facilities for housing Native American juveniles in America in 1989 and found 22 attempted suicides and one completed suicide in these facilities (whose capacity was 66 inmates). In a survey of 17 adult and adult-plus-juvenile facilities, one reported an adult completed suicide in the past year, and 81 percent reported at least one adult suicide attempt (average 1.6). Fifty-seven percent reported at least one juvenile suicide attempt (average 1.7).

Simpson et al. (1983) studied the Hopi Indian Reservation for 1979 to 1980 and found 38 completed and attempted suicides, eleven of which occurred in jail in people arrested for intoxication. Nine of the eleven used hanging.

Grossman (1992) noted that in the Canadian federal prison for women (housing about 110 women, one-quarter of whom were Native Canadians), six Native Canadian women committed suicide in two years. Grossman examined the two major theories about suicide in prison for their relevance for Native Canadian women: deprivation theories (the prison itself causes the suicides) and importation theories (the prisoner has certain traits that make suicide more likely).

Relevant to deprivation theories, Grossman noted that the social isolation of prison, both from the home community and, if the inmate is placed in isolation in the prison, from the other prisoners, may be especially difficult for Native Canadian women to cope with. There is racism and discrimination for the Native Canadian women, both from the staff and other inmates. Even the helping services available are culturally white-oriented rather than culturally Native Canadian-oriented. The Native Canadian women lose control over their destiny, like other female inmates, but perhaps suffer more shame and social disgrace in the eyes of their home communities.

Relevant to importation theories, Grossman noted that Native Canadian women are the most disadvantaged group in Canada, worse off than Native Canadian men. They have less education, more unemployment, earn less when employed (and those who cannot pay fines are more likely to be imprisoned), have a higher suicide rate in the community than white women in Canada, and often have a history of physical and sexual abuse both as children and as adults. Indeed, Grossman noted that the rate of Native Canadian women murdering husbands has increased in recent years, while the same behavior in white women has not.

Adjustment to Prison

Adjustment to prison life may be difficult for Native Americans. Tyler and Thompson (1965) reported on the case of a Navajo woman in the 1930s convicted of murdering a relative. She was unable to converse with fellow inmates and staff because she could not speak English. She became depressed and resistive. She vomited and refused to eat. She was transferred to a psychiatric institution in the East, where she spoke to no one for many years and lay huddled in the fetal position in a blanket on the floor. During the next twenty years she showed improvement, spoke her native language, ate and slept well, and was quiet and pleasant. After twenty years, a social caseworker helped her return to the Navajo reservation and become involved with her family there.

On the other hand, Everett (1970) noted that, while most White Mountain Apache do not like being incarcerated, a good percentage adapt to confinement quite well, reacting with an "eager resignation." Jail provides a fairly secure and comfortable respite from the stress of everyday life.

French (1979) noted that, while prison may be traumatic for all inmates, the type and extent of trauma may vary with orientation of the inmate. For Native Americans, French classified them as traditional, middle-class and marginal. French felt that marginals are more likely to violate majority norms and get arrested, but that traditionals may find prison more traumatic, especially if they are not permitted to maintain their values.

Religious Freedom

Grobsmith (1994) documented that changes instituted in the Nebraska prison system which were the result of the Nebraska Consent Decree and the passage of the 1978 American Indian Religious Freedom Act.[3] Nebraska has a relatively large Native American prison population, 3.6 percent in August, 1992, all of whom

---

3. For a good examination of the rights of Native American prisoners in this regard see Holscher (1992).

had committed off-reservation crimes.[4] The majority are members of the various Sioux tribes (Oglala, Brulé, Santee and Yankton), with some Omaha, Winnebago, Chippewa and Ponca. Once in prison, however, the particular tribal affiliation takes a backseat to the more inclusive label of "Native American."

As a result of the consent decree (CV 72-L-156, Order Designating Class Action, Nov. 21, 1973), the Native Americans in the system won the rights to certain religious freedoms in the system.[5] As a result, since then, they have litigated in the courts for privileges under the terms of this consent decree. Although many of the suits have been lost, some have been settled out of court, occasional suits won, and, most importantly, a process set up to handle disputes. Other states have studied the Nebraska situation in order to learn how better to handle similar problems in their prison systems.

The litigation filed in Nebraska in recent years has involved disputes over the use of sweat lodges, problems with admitting spiritual leaders and medicine men to the prisons, which inmates have access to the sweat lodges, the lack of consistency in Native American Studies curricula, the hiring of sufficient Native American staff and the privileges of Native American groups and clubs.[6]

French (1979) has reported the establishment by Native Americans of a voluntary prerelease Native American run correctional facility for five northern plains states in order to help Native American prisoners. The first such program, the Swift Bird Project in South Dakota, began in 1979 on the Cheyenne River Sioux Reservation, but lasted only two years before it closed because of internal problems (mismanagement, personality clashes and lack of funding). However, other programs have been established, such as the Minnesota Anishinabe Longhouse (Peak, 1989).

Despite these innovative programs in some states, other states continue to ignore the rights of prisoners. Reed (1989) has described his struggles in the Ohio prison system to obtain the freedom to practice religion and documented the prejudice toward Native American prisoners by the administrators of the system.

---

4. On-reservation crime is handled by tribal and federal agencies.
5. The Native American Rights Fund also instituted lawsuits against nine states and the federal prison in Lompoc, California, in order to secure rights for Native American prisoners to practice their traditional religion (Mann, 1993).
6. Oklahoma State Prison in the late 1980s was still forbidding Native American religious practices (Young et al., 1987).

Thunderhorse (1989) described an alliance that had been formed to coordinate the various groups of Native Americans in and out of prison working to change prison conditions for Native Americans–the Thunderbird Prison Alliance–which eventually formed a nonprofit corporation and an indigenous tribal council. *The Alliance* publishes a newsletter and books and tries to inform those concerned about networking, forming prison circles, and opportunities for Native American prisoners.

Problems of Competing Jurisdictions

Humphrey (1985) provided an interesting example, of the ambiguities created by the different jurisdictional authorities for Native American inmates. A young Native American man was arrested for rape on the reservation. The U.S. Attorney's Office declined to prosecute, and so the offense was downgraded to a misdemeanor and heard before the tribal court. He was convicted and sentenced to four years in jail. After several months in the tribal jail, it was clear that the offender was psychiatrically disturbed. Two psychologists agreed that he needed commitment to a psychiatric facility, which in this case was state-run. The state facility, however, would only accept a voluntary commitment by the offender or involuntary ordered by the county court. The county court claimed, rightly, that it had no authority in the case.

The problem was solved by a chance incident. A county sheriff's officer was helping out at the jail as a result of tribal-county agreement and was assaulted by the prisoner. This enabled charges to be filed in the county court which then ordered the prisoner to the state facility where he was stabilized on medication.[7] Humphrey noted that psychiatrically disturbed Native Americans often receive no treatment until they commit crimes and are processed through the criminal justice system.

Inappropriate Detention of Juveniles

Bond-Maupin et al. (1995) studied the disposition of juveniles on a Native American reservation in the southwest, home to some 7,000

---

7. After the prisoner was returned to the tribal jail and released on probation, he violated the terms of his probation and "disappeared."

Native Americans. There is a tribal court, and the detention center was built by the Bureau of Indian Affairs in 1985. Funds to operate the facility were made available in 1987, with one staff member, two bureau police officers for security (mainly from different Native American tribes). The facility was modeled on maximum security adult facilities

A survey of the juveniles revealed that 74 percent of the offenses were for minor delinquency or status offenses. Nine percent were "children in need of care." Sixty-four percent were awaiting a preliminary hearing and 27 percent awaiting judgment. Forty-three percent stayed more than two days.

The conclusion was obvious. The Bureau of Indian Affairs was punishing Native American youths by incarceration for primarily minor offenses. Why? The reasons include lack of personnel, lack of tribal involvement, and the lack of alternative meaningful resources for a community spread out over a large reservation.

The situation improved in 1990 after the tribe took over the administration of the facility (Bond-Maupin, 1996). Services for detained youths increased, including prevention, probation and aftercare services, and the institution came to resemble a proper juvenile correctional facility. Eighty-three percent of the youths in 1990 were awaiting a detention or adjudication hearing, and the average length of stay was 11 days with a modal stay of one day. However, although a smaller proportion of youths were detained in the facility prior to a hearing than prior to 1990, detention was increasingly used as a disposition (14% up from 4%). Twenty-five percent of the adjudicated cases were dismissed. Bond-Maupin concluded that, although the detention center had improved, punitive justice was still being meted out to the Native American youths, now by their own tribe who appeared to have adopted the punitive perspective of the Bureau of Indian Affairs.

Probation and Parole

Mills (1989) noted the high incidence of alcoholism among Native American offenders and pointed out that this poses serious problems for the probation and parole officer. This is made worse by the fact that often Native Americans living on reservations have very few resources available for treating alcohol abuse and that the poor living conditions on the reservation provide little incentive to remain sober.

Red Horse et al. (1978) noted the importance for probation officers and courts to become aware of cultural differences. As an example, they described the case of a young male probationer who was ordered to remain with responsible adults. He appeared to ignore this order, moved around frequently, and stayed overnight with different young women. At a staff meeting, fellow staff stated their suspicion that he was a drug pusher or a pimp. The young women appeared to know one another and enjoy one another's company, and they seemed quite willing to appear in public together with the probationer. The probation counselor initiated violation proceedings.

Luckily, a Native American professional came across the case accidentally. He asked that the court proceedings be delayed and investigated. He found out that the young women were all first cousins to the probationer and, rather than behaving frivolously, he had been staying with different units of his family. Each home that he visited had a responsible adult to supervise and care for the young man if needed. The young man in fact had a family network of over 200 people spanning three generations.

The point is clear. Criminal justice staff working with Native Americans need to be trained in and sensitive to the cultural customs and practices of the different Native American tribes. More importantly, Native Americans should be recruited into the criminal justice system so that they can work directly with offenders.[8]

Comment

This chapter has documented the poor facilities provided for rehabilitation of Native American prisoners in state and federal prisons, especially given the high rate of alcohol addiction present in this group. Native Americans have also suffered as a result of the inadequate facilities and staffing in police lock-ups, jails and local prisons which are used to incarcerate Native Americans. The incompetence of those responsible for these problems is clear, and the intransigence of those failing to remedy these faults reprehensible.

---

8. Reasons (1976) has called this approach a conflict/pluralist policy as opposed to a order/assimilationist policy.

REFERENCES

Benjamin, R., & Kim, C. N. American Indians and the criminal justice system. *Criminal Justice Abstracts*, 1980, *12*, 314-315.

Bond-Maupin, L. J. Who made the code in the first place? *Crime, Law & Social Change*, 1996, *25*, 133-152.

Bond-Maupin, L. J., Lujan, C. C., & Bortner, M. A. Jailing of American Indian adolescents. *Crime, Law & Social Change*, 1995, *23*, 1-16.

Duclos, C. W., LeBeau, W., & Elias, G. L. American Indian adolescent suicidal behavior in detention environments. *American Indian & Alaska Native Mental Health Research*, 1994a, 4, monograph, 189-221.

Duclos, C. W., LeBeau, W., & Elias, G. L. American Indian suicidal behavior in detention environments. *Jail Suicide Update*, 1994b, *5*(4), 4-9.

Everett, M. W. Pathology in White Mountain Apache culture. *Western Canadian Journal of Anthropology*, 1970, *2*, 180-203.

Flaherty, M. G. The national incidence of juvenile suicide in adult jails and juvenile detention centers. *Suicide & Life-Threatening Behavior*, 1983, *13*, 85-94.

Flowers, R. B. *Minorities and criminality*. Westport, CT: Greenwood, 1990

French, L. Corrections and the Native American client. *Prison Journal*, 1979, *59*(1), 49-60.

Grobsmith, E. S. *Indians in prison*. Lincoln, NE: University of Nebraska Press, 1994.

Grossman, M. G. Two perspectives on aboriginal female suicides in custody. *Canadian Journal of Criminology*, 1992, *34*, 403-416.

Holscher, L. M. Sweat lodges and headbands. *New England Journal on Criminal & Civil Confinement*, 1992, *18*(1-2), 33-62.

Humphrey, G. W. Civil commitment of Indian persons. *White Cloud Journal*, 1985, *3*(4), 27-30.

Lane, E. B., Daniels, H. W., Blyan, J. D., & Royer, R. The incarcerated native. *Canadian Journal of Criminology*, 1978, *20*, 308-316.

LaPrairie, C. P. Selected criminal justice and sociodemographic data on Native women. *Canadian Journal of Criminology*, 1984, *26*, 161-170.

Lester, D., & Danto, B. L. *Suicide behind bars*. Philadelphia: Charles Press, 1993.

Mann, C. R. *Unequal justice*. Indianapolis, IN: University of Indiana, 1993.

Martin, M. D. A look at Indian jails. *American Jails*, 1988, Spring, 19-21.

Mills, D. K. Alcohol and crime on the reservation. *Federal Probation*, 1989, *53*(4), 12-15.

Peak, K. Criminal justice, law, and policy in Indian country. *Journal of Criminal Justice*, 1989, *17*, 393-407.

Reasons, C. E. Native offenders and correctional policy. *Crime and/et Justice*, 1976, *4*(4), 255-267.

Red Horse, J. G., Lewis, R., Feit, M., & Decker, J. Family behavior of urban American Indians. *Social Casework*, 1978, *59*(2), 67-72.

Reed, L. R. The American Indian in the white man's prisons. *Humanity & Society*, 1989, *13*, 403-420.

Simpson, S. G., Reid, R., Baker, S. P., & Teret, S. Injuries among the Hopi Indians. *Journal of the American Medical Association*, 1983, *249*, 1873-1876.

Thunderhorse, I. The Thunderbird Alliance. *Humanity & Society*, 1989, *13*, 421-427.

Tyler, I. M., & Thompson, S. D. Cultural factors in casework treatment of a Navajo mental patient. *Social Casework*, 1965, *46*, 215-220.

Young, T. J., LaPlante, C., & Robbins, W. Indians before the law. *Quarterly Journal of Ideology*, 1987, *11*(4), 59-70.

Chapter 15

DISCRIMINATION IN THE CRIMINAL JUSTICE SYSTEM

Native Americans feel that they have been and continue to be discriminated against by the criminal justice system. Bahr, et al. (1972) surveyed Native Americans in Seattle, and found that they felt discriminated against in housing, employment, welfare and social services, the health professions and the police. Two-thirds of Native Americans felt that police were "often unnecessarily brutal to Indians they arrest" versus only a quarter of whites. The majority of Native Americans felt that the police use derogatory language against them more than against whites, that they use excessive force more often, and that they are not consistently fair to Native Americans. Eighteen percent asserted that they had been arrested primarily because they were Native Americans. This perception of discrimination applied to the court system as well.

Bahr gave an example:

> We were at this place and these cops came and there was this car there and we just happened to be there—there was about six of us, mostly Indians. And they said that, well, we weren't really doing anything. I think they were going to turn us loose, but this one guy said, "Well, let's take them down to the station and say we picked them up for prowling...."
>
> I went over to a policeman and told him that I was bleeding internally and to take me to the hospital, but instead he took me to jail because he thought I was drunk....(p. 8).

Racial disparities in sentencing have commonly been documented in the United States, but most of the research has compared the way in which African American offenders are treated as compared to white offenders. There are many reasons why Native Americans may be discriminated against in the criminal justice system (Hall and Simkus, 1975). They have less power and influence than whites, they may be victims of negative ethnic stereotyping, and they are often in social and economic conflict with the ruling whites.

It has been noted that Native Americans (and Native Canadians) are present in prisons with a higher frequency than their proportion in the population would warrant (e.g., Anon, 1990-1991) and that their arrests rates are high for some crimes. Petterson (1972) noted that in one rural Minnesota county (Cass County), 80 percent of the probationers in 1967 were Native Americans whereas Native Americans made up only ten percent of the county population. Nine percent of the youths in Minnesota's correctional facilities were Native Americans in 1969 whereas they comprise only one percent of the state population.

These simple statistics are not sufficient to show discrimination because they do not take into account possible differences between the offenders from different ethnic groups, such as economic status. There are some better studies which have explored whether discrimination toward Native Americans exists in the criminal justice system, and these will be reviewed in the present chapter.

Arrests

Luebben (1964) studied "Carbonate City" in Colorado, where the zinc mines employed both whites and Native Americans. In 1953, the 117 of the 335 residents were Native Americans, and 34 of the 102 adult males were Native Americans (33%). From 1946 to 1954, 146 males appeared in police magistrate court, of whom 122 (84%) were Navajos. These 122 Native Americans involved 88 different Navajos since several of them appeared in court more than once.

In 25 cases, the complainant was a Navajo, and in nine of these cases the complainant was a Navajo female. No white females filed complaints. For example, one complaint was filed by a sister-in-law, and three wives accused their husbands of misconduct. Luebben suggested that traditional means for resolving disputes among the Navajo were not available to these off-reservation Navajos, and so they turned to the legal system for help in resolving disputes.

Of the 122 Navajo arrests, 98 involved offenses against the public peace—disturbing the peace, fighting or being drunk and disorderly.

Five traffic violations and eight unclassifiable violations made up the rest of the complaints. For most of this period, it was forbidden to sell alcohol to Native Americans.[1] Suppliers of bootleg alcohol were rarely apprehended, and the fining of Native Americans was seen by a few officials as treating the symptom rather than the cause.[2]

Following arrest, most defendants were found guilty: 88 percent of the Navajos and 91 percent of the whites. The same proportion pled guilty (37 percent of the Navajos and 36 percent of the whites), and the fines assessed were similar. However, the four judges involved showed different patterns of decision-making, even though overall the differences balanced one another. The conclusion appears to be that there was no evidence for discrimination in the arrests and sentencing in this community.

Lundman (1974) rode with police officers in a midwestern city for fifteen months and 1970 and 1971 and observed 195 encounters with people who were publicly drunk. He eliminated cases in which a felony was involved or where the drunken person was driving a motor vehicle. Thirty-one percent of the 195 encounters resulted in an arrest. An arrest was more likely if the police initiated the encounter, if the encounter was downtown, if it was in closed public place and if the drunk was male and over the age of 25. An arrest was also more likely if the drunk was a Native American. Fifty-three percent of the Native Americans were arrested, but only 33 percent of the African Americans and 26 percent of the whites. Native American encounters more often occurred downtown and involved more complaints, but controls for these variables, as well as the disrespect shown by the drunk (impoliteness and noncompliance) did not eliminate the bias toward Native Americans.

Lundman speculated that police arrest Native Americans more because such arrests are less "risky," by which he meant that, in arrests of Native Americans, there is less risk of an accusation of false arrest, a public scene or bad publicity because Native Americans are powerless in the society.

Wordes and Bynum (1995) studied nine jurisdictions in Michigan and found that, while Native American youths were not overrepresented in police records as a whole, they were more likely to be dis-

---

1. The prohibition was repealed on August 15, 1953.
2. Luebben suggested that theft was not uncommon among the Navajos, but no Navajo was accused of theft, and Luebben presented no data to support this suggestion.

proportionately represented at the more formal intervention stages in the law enforcement process (such as referred to court for status offenses). However, Wordes and Bynum introduced no controls for criminal or personal background.[3]

In a study of juveniles in Minnesota in 1986, Schwartz et al. (1988) found that Native Americans were held for longer periods of time in county jails than were whites for both Part I and Part II offenses, but for less time for probation and parole violations. They did, not, however, control for other variables.

Fisher and Doyle-Martin (1981) studied referrals to a juvenile court in a southwestern town in 1977 to 1979. Referrals by police officers could be "physical," in which situation the juvenile was brought in person to the court, or "paper," in which situation the police officer let the juvenile go but filed a written complaint with the court. Fisher and Doyle-Martin found that making a physical referral was more common if the juvenile had three or more prior referrals and if the offense was serious. The effect of age differed for white and African American juveniles, but not studied for Native American juveniles. All minorities were more likely to receive a physical referral, especially Native American youths, even after controls for the other variables.

Plea Negotiation

Hartnagel (1975) looked at cases from the files of a Canadian prairie city in 1973 to 1973 and found that plea negotiation occurred in 28 percent of the cases—29 percent of whites but only 16 percent of the Native Canadians. Plea negotiation was more likely if the offender had no previous record (especially for Native Canadians), if the offender had multiple charges (but not for Native Canadians), and if the offense was an indictable offense rather than a summary offense (but not for Native Canadians). Thus, the factors affecting plea negotiation varied by ethnicity.

Zatz et al. (1991) suggested that Native Americans may plead guilty more than white defendants because they may be unfamiliar and uncomfortable with the court, may lack confidence in whether they will get a fair trial, are uncertain over their ability to communicate to their attorney or the judge the relevant aspects of their case, and desire

---

3. Native American youths were present in only one of the eight districts and all were picked up by the police for status offenses.

to get the process over with as quickly as possible. They may also have difficulties communicating in English to the court personnel.

Sentencing

Studies Reporting Ethnic Differences

Hall and Simkus (1975) studied all offenders sentenced to probationary types of sentences for felonies between 1966 and 1972 in one western state. The sentences could be deferred sentences, entirely suspended sentences or partially suspended sentences after a short stay in prison. Native American offenders were less likely to receive deferred sentences than white offenders but more likely to receive partially suspended sentences. Native Americans, therefore, went to prison more than whites.

Native Americans and whites committed different types of offenses —Native Americans had more often committed forgery, burglary, assault and auto theft while the whites had more often committed drug offenses, grand larceny, and using false checks. However, even after controls for the type of offense and other variables (including the number of prior felonies, the length of sentence, juvenile offenses, juvenile institutionalization, education, employment, occupation, marital status, age and sex), the ethnic difference remained except for those with juvenile records and institutionalization, prior felony convictions and aged 30 to 39.[4]

In a second study, Hall and Simkus (1975) studied a one-year cohort of offenders sentenced for felonies between 1966 and 1967. The pattern was similar to the previous study, with Native Americans less likely to receive a deferred sentence and more likely to serve time in prison (partially or for the full sentence). In this data set, a full multiple regression still showed an effect from ethnicity ($p = .06$).

Hall and Simkus suggested that the Native American's powerlessness, negative stereotypes (such as "drunken, brawling Indians"), increased visibility off the reservation, and low social and economic status may contribute to this discrimination in the criminal justice system. Native Americans may be less able to hire competent lawyers, raise bail, or negotiate pleas effectively. Judges may see reservations as

---

4. These variables were studied one at a time and not with a multiple regression technique.

less conducive to successful completion of probation, making Native Americans poor risks for such dispositions. Since the Native Americans were arrested off the reservation, their offenses were probably against whites, making them appear to be a great threat to the white community.

Interviews with judges suggested that the Native Americans often displayed a poor "attitude" in court, showing poor respect for the court, having a bad demeanor, and not expressing guilt or remorse for their crimes. The judges relied heavily on reports from probation officers, and so much of the discrimination may lie with the probation officers rather than the judges.

Interviews with Native American offenders suggested that they do feel discriminated against and persecuted by whites and by the criminal justice system. This may affect their attitude in court which in turn may lead to harsher treatment, a circular process.

Hood and Harlan (1991) studied sentencing in Yakima County (Washington) in 1986 to 1989–both the total incarceration time and authorized work release. The verdicts were arrived by guilty pleas from all 104 Native American defendants, but only 96.6 percent of white defendants and 94.2 percent of Hispanic defendants. Compared to whites, Native Americans received similar sentences, but both of these groups received shorter sentences than Hispanics. Controlling for gender and age, whites received shorter sentences by two days over Native Americans and eight days over Hispanics. Whites received three times the work release of Hispanics, but did not differ from Native Americans. Controls for age and sex did not change these differences.

In a second study, extending for a longer period (1986 to 1991), Hood and Lin (1993), these differences were replicated.[5] In this latter study, controls for type of crime were introduced, as well as age and sex. For burglary, whites received sentence three days less than Native Americans and nine days less than Hispanics. Exceptional sentences (that is, outside the recommended range, which must be supported by a written statement from the judge) were more often for longer sentences for Native Americans and Hispanics than for whites. Hood and Lin noted that Hispanics committed far more drug offences than Native Americans or whites. Overall, therefore, Hispanics received

---

5. The difference in guilty pleas between Native Americans and whites was much less for this extended period (96.9% versus 95.6%).

harsher sentences than Native Americans and whites. Native Americans did not differ much in their sentences from whites but, where differences emerged, the sentences of Native Americans tended to be a little longer than those for whites.

Poupart (1995) studied court records for juveniles in two Wisconsin counties with a fair proportion of Native Americans for 1986 to 1990. She looked at four decision points: the decision to refer the case to the prosecutor at intake, the detention decision, whether a delinquency petition was filed, and the disposition of the case. She found that Native American youths were more often referred to the prosecutor than were white youths (63% versus 39%), were more often detained (15% versus 7%), did not more often have a delinquency petition filed (99% versus 100%), but were more severely treated (for example, 24% versus 11% transferred to a juvenile facility or waived into adult court). However, Poupart did not examine the role any other variables (such as the social class of the youths, prior records, or representation in court) in these decisions.

Mixed Results

Alvarez and Bachman (1996) studied the inmates in Arizona state correctional facilities in 1990, a sample which included Native Americans committing felonies off the reservation.[6] Whites received longer sentence lengths for assault, sexual assault, and homicide, Native Americans received longer sentences for burglary, and there was no difference in sentence length for larceny. Multiple regressions controlling for prior felony record, age, sex, and educational level confirmed these differences. Alvarez and Bachman speculated that crimes against persons were typically intraracial, and so Native Americans probably assaulted and killed other Native Americans whereas they probably stole from whites. The race of the victim, therefore, might account for the disparities in sentences, with white victims resulting in longer sentences. However, Alvarez and Bachman had no data on the ethnicity of the victim, and so their speculation had no basis in fact.

Bachman et al. (1996) studied sentence length and time served for major crimes by Native Americans and whites in California, Minnesota, North Carolina, North Dakota and Arizona in 1990. In

---

6. Tribal courts handle misdemeanors while federal courts handle felonies committed on the reservations.

general, Native Americans received longer sentences for robbery, burglary, drug trafficking and public order offenses, shorter sentences for larceny, and similar sentences for murder, assault and sexual assault. However, the results varied by state. North Carolina was the most discriminatory state, while North Dakota showed reverse discrimination. In terms of the proportion of the sentence served, Minnesota and North Carolina were the most discriminatory toward Native Americans, while California showed reverse discrimination. The problem with drawing firm conclusions from these data from Bachman et al. is that the researchers failed to control for any other variables, such as prior convictions and infractions incurred during the period of imprisonment.

Feld (1995) looked at the juvenile court records in Hennepin County in Minnesota for the year 1986. He noted that a greater proportion of the Native American youths appeared in court for status offenses than did white or African American youth. In multiple regressions, controlling for offense severity, prior record, and prior removal from home, Feld found that being African American or Native American increased the chances of being represented by counsel,[7] of being detained, and of having a disposition involving removal from the home. However, there were no racial differences in commitment to secure institutions.

In a study of pre-sentence reports in Alberta in 1973, Hagan (1977) found no effect of ethnicity in urban areas. However, in rural areas, the pre-sentence reports more often recommended severe sentences for the Native Canadians. The major factor affecting the severity of the recommendation in urban areas was prior record, and the Native Canadians did have more prior convictions than the whites. In the rural areas, ethnicity had a direct effect on the recommendation. The Native Canadians were more likely to end up in prison in the rural areas than whites and less often fined.

Bynum and Paternoster (1984) studied a cohort of offenders admitted to the state prison of an upper plains state in 1970. They excluded prisoners not eligible for release during the period of the study and "singular" offenses such as child molestation and extortion. The sam-

---

7. White youths were more likely to have private counsel while Native American and African Americans were more likely to have the public defender representing them. For felony offenses against the person, Native Americans were as likely as whites to have private counsel, but for felony offenses involving property, Native American youths were less likely than African Americans youths to have private counsel.

ple consisted of 137 offenders, of whom 54 were Native Americans. They found that the Native Americans had significantly shorter sentences imposed (18.6 months versus 26.5 months), a difference that was apparent even when the sample was restricted to only burglars. This difference was found even after controls for age, education and prior convictions. However, looking at the percentage of the sentence served, the Native Americans served significantly greater percentages than the whites (86% versus 75%) even after controls for the length of sentence and other variables (age, education and prior convictions).

Bynum and Paternoster speculated that Native Americans may have had a poorer demeanor at the parole board hearings and have been perceived as having less community support (including prospects for employment and stable living arrangements). However, they also suggested that the authorities make an effort not to discriminate against Native Americans in the public setting ("frontstage"), but do display their discriminatory tendencies in private settings ("backstage").

Benjamin and Kim (1980) studied 14,203 cases processed in Minnesota from 1973 to 1975, including all Native Americans and African Americans arrested and a 2.5 percent sample of all whites arrested. Controlling for population size, Native Americans were 2.53 times as likely to be arrested than were whites. Native Americans were arrested more often than whites for robbery, assault, burglary, larceny, auto theft, driving under the influence, disorderly conduct and violating liquor laws, and these crimes were committed primarily by juveniles.

A greater proportion of Native Americans were held after arrest than were whites (43% versus 22%), and fewer released on bail (36% versus 55%). The Native Americans were less likely to hire a private attorney (15% versus 32%), were more likely to have the case dismissed (23% versus 19%), but did not differ in guilty pleas (84% versus 86%) or convictions (42% versus 44%). Thus, although there seemed to be some discrimination in the earlier stages of the process, the outcomes were similar for Native Americans and whites.[8] The whites had the charges against them dropped earlier in the process than Native Americans. Race did not affect the maximum sentence the offenders received or early releases.

However, with regard to sentencing, Native Americans were sentenced to probation less often than whites (32% versus 51%) but were

---

8. These differences seemed to hold up for most offense categories.

fined more often (24% versus 10%) and imprisoned more often (36% versus 25%). Native Americans served more time in prison than whites but less time on probation. Native Americans also had a greater proportion of stayed or suspended sentences (36% versus 28%).

Reverse Discrimination

Leiber (1994) studied the processing of defendants in a juvenile court in Iowa during 1980 to 1989, taking into account twelve control variables. The Native Americans were treated more leniently than African Americans and whites at intake[9] and at the petition stage, but there were no differences at the initial appearance or judicial disposition stages. The Native American youth were more often diverted, and this was probably due to the presence in the community of the Indian Youth of America, an agency specializing in handling Native American youth.

Feimer et al. (1990) noted that 24 percent of inmates in South Dakota prisons were Native Americans as compared to only 8 percent of the population. To explore whether this excess of Native Americans among the prison population was a result of discrimination, they studied all white and Native American prisoners incarcerated between January 1, 1985, and June 30, 1985, who were still in prison when the study was conducted. The two groups were similar in age and education, but the Native American prisoners were less often married, less often had a juvenile record, were more often in prison for an alcohol-related offense, and had worked for shorter periods of time. The Native Americans were in prison more for burglary, possession of stolen goods, escape and driving while intoxicated; they were in prison less often for rape, sexual contact with a child and grand theft.

There were no differences in the length of sentence, with the whites having sightly longer sentences than the Native Americans (6.5 years versus 5.7 years). However, the punishment severity, defined as the percentage of the maximum sentence possible, was significantly less for the Native Americans than for the whites (48% versus 54%). This difference, favoring the Native Americans, was found only for prisoners with one or zero previous convictions. For two or more convic-

---

9. Older Native American youth were treated less leniently at this stage, but Native American drug offenders were treated more leniently at this stage.

tions, there was no difference in the punishment severity between Native Americans and whites.

In multiple regression analyses, the predictors of punishment severity were race, age, number of convictions and having prior felonies. For the whites, age, number of prior convictions, number of prior felonies and using a weapon predicted punishment severity, while only having prior felonies predicted punishment severity for the Native Americans. Thus, in this study, there was no evidence for discrimination against Native Americans.

No Differences

Bienvenue and Latif (1974) studied the arrests of adult Native Canadians[10] in Winnipeg City in 1969. Although they comprised only three percent of the urban population, 27 percent of the male arrests and 69 percent of the females arrests were Native Canadians, with 41 percent and 78 percent of the arrests of the men and women being respectively for liquor offenses. Bienvenue and Latif reported that there were no differences between the Native Canadians and the whites in prior arrests or in dispositions.

Boldt et al. (1983) studied presentence reports and eventual sentences in the Yukon in 1980. They found that the judges followed the sentencing recommendations of the probation officers in 85 percent of the cases but, when they differed, were usually harsher. The Native Canadians were more likely to be incarcerated than whites (40% versus 30%), but this difference was accounted for by two factors–the Native Canadians had more prior convictions and had committed more serious crimes. Thus, race per se had no significant effect on disposition. Boldt did note, however, that imposition of a fine more often resulted in incarceration for Native Canadians than for whites since Native Canadians frequently could not pay the fine.

Pommersheim and Wise (1989) studied the entrance sheets of male inmates to the South Dakota prison system from 1981 to mid-1985. Considering only crimes for which there were white and Native American prisoners, their sample included 409 whites and 148 Native Americans. The severity of the sentence was defined as the percentage of the maximum sentence given to the prisoner, and white and Native

---

10. "Native Canadian" includes those labeled at Indians and Metis by the Canadians. Metis are of mixed ancestry.

American received the sentences of the same severity, even after controls for prior felony convictions,[11] crime type, or judge. Indeed, in the only difference that approached significance, Native Americans received less severe sentences. Thus, although there was a greater proportion of native Americans in the prison system than their proportion in the population would predict, their sentences were not more severe than those of white prisoners.

Hutton et al. (1989) examined all women sentenced to the state penitentiary in South Dakota from 1980 to 1988. The Native American women and white women were similar in marital status, juvenile record and prior convictions for felonies. The Native American women were a little older and less educated. Looking at the felony crimes, and taking into account the number of years suspended, the two groups of women were sentenced to almost the same percentage of the maximum sentence (44.3% for the whites versus 45.0% for the Native Americans). Thus, there was no evidence of sentencing disparity for these convicted female felons.

Hagan (1975) studied a Canadian midwestern city and examined 1,018 cases involving 1,500 charges in a six month period. There were no differences between whites and Native Canadians in whether a defense counsel was retained, whether they entered a plea of not guilty or whether the primary charge was altered. Ethnicity was also not associated with having the charge dismissed or with the sentence (fine, probation or prison). The Native Canadians did have more prior arrests than whites and were of lower socioeconomic status, and these two variables did have some impact with the outcome, but ethnicity itself did not.

Disparities in the Law

MacMeekin (1969) noted one historical disparity in the law. A Native American who rapes a non-Native American on the reservation can be executed, while a Native American who rapes a Native American woman on the reservation cannot, a difference upheld by *Gray v. United States* (394 F.2d 96 [9th Cir. 1968]). According to the statutes in force at the time, the death penalty was possible for anyone raping a non-Native American female, and the Gray court argued that

---

11. The Native Americans did not have more prior felony convictions than the whites.

the law operated in favor of Native Americans by treating Native American men more leniently (if, as MacMeekin pointed out, they have "exclusively Indian tastes").

Prison

Bonta (1989) studied 126 prisoners in Ontario jails whose sentences ranged from 90 days to two years less one day.[12] The Native Canadians and non-Natives did not differ in sentence length, nor in recommendations for halfway houses or treatment. The two groups did not differ in security classification and security decisions, in parole rate and length of sentence served, in institutional behavior (including misconduct and assault), in recidivism after release or parole violations.[13]

Comment

The surprising conclusion from the studies reviewed in this chapter is that Native Americans do not appear to suffer unduly from discrimination in the criminal justice system. Occasional reports do find discrimination, but occasional reports find reverse discrimination, while the majority of studies find mixed results or no differences.

It is important to note also that some of the research reviewed here was quite poor methodologically. Very few factors were controlled for in the analyses, such as criminal justice factors (e.g., criminal history of the defendant or representation in court) and background variables (e.g., age of defendant, social class, and education). Furthermore, some of the studies did not utilize multiple regression statistical techniques. Of those studies employing controls for other variables, seven studies reported discrimination against Native Americans, two studies reported discrimination in favor of Native Americans, six studies reported mixed results and six studies found no differences at all.

The arbitrary nature of the results is noteworthy. Assuming that the differences reported do stand up after better research is carried out, the discrimination faced by Native Americans in the criminal justice appears to vary greatly from region to region. For example, in the study by Bachman et al. (1996), some states showed some discrimina-

---

12. If the sentence is longer than this, the prisoner is transferred to a federal prison.
13. Financial difficulties predicted parole violations and recidivism for non-Natives, while alcohol and drug abuse problems predicted these for Native Canadians

tion while others showed less or even reverse discrimination. The sentence meted out to an offender for a given crime should not depend upon the region of the United States where that crime is committed.

REFERENCES

Alvarez, A., & Bachman, R. D. American Indians and sentencing disparity. *Journal of Criminal Justice*, 1996, *24*, 549-561.

Anon. *Statistical profile on Native Mental Health.* Ottawa: Indian & Northern Health Services, 1990-1991.

Bachman, R., Alvarez, A., & Perkins, C. Discriminatory imposition of the law. In M. O. Nielsen & R. A. Silverman (Eds.) *Native Americans, crime and justice*, pp. 197-208. Boulder, CO: Westview, 1996.

Bahr, H. M., Chadwick, B. A., & Stauss, J. H. Discrimination against urban Indians in Seattle. *Indian Historian*, 1972, *5*, (Winter), 4-11.

Benjamin, R., & Kim, C. N. American Indians and the criminal justice system. *Criminal Justice Abstracts*, 1980, *12*, 314-315.

Bienvenue, P. M., & Latif, A. H. Arrests, dispositions and recidivism. *Canadian Journal of Criminology*, 1974, *16*, 105-116.

Boldt, E. D., Hursh, L. E., Johnson, S. D., & Taylor, K. W. Presentence reports and the incarceration of Natives. *Canadian Journal of Criminology*, 1983, *25*, 269-276.

Bonta, J. Native inmates. *Canadian Journal of Criminology*, 1989, *31*, 49-62.

Bynum, T. S., & Paternoster, R. Discrimination revisited. *Sociology & Social Research*, 1984, *69*, 90-108.

Feimer, S., Pommersheim, F., & Wise, S. Marking time. *Journal of Crime & Justice*, 1990, *13*(1), 86-102.

Feld, B. C. The social context of juvenile justice administration. In K. K. Leonard, C. E., Pope & W. H. Feyerherm (Eds.), *Minorities in juvenile justice*, pp. 66-97. Thousand Oaks, CA: Sage, 1995.

Fisher, G. A., & Doyle-Martin, S. M. The effect of ethnic prejudice on police referrals to the juvenile court. *California Sociologist*, 1918, *4*, 189-205.

Hagan, J. Parameters of criminal prosecution. *Journal of Criminal Law & Criminology*, 1975, *65*, 536-544.

Hagan, J. Criminal justice in rural and urban communities. *Social Forces*, 1977, *55*, 597-611.

Hall, E., & Simkus, A. Inequality in the type of sentences received by Native Americans and whites. *Criminology*, 1975, *13*, 199-222.

Hartnagel, T. F. Plea negotiation in Canada. *Canadian Journal of Criminology*, 1975, *17*, 45-56.

Hood, D. L., & Harlan, J. R. Ethnic disparities in sentencing and the Washington Sentencing Reform Act. *Explorations in Ethnics Studies*, 1991, *14*, 43-55.

Hood, D. L., & Lin, R. L. Sentencing disparity in Yakima County. *Explorations in Ethnics Studies*, 1993, *16*, 99-114.

Hutton, C., Pommersheim, F., & Feimer, S. I fought the law and the law won. *New England Journal of Criminal & Civil Confinement,* 1989, *15,* 177-201.

Leiber, M. J. A comparison of juvenile court outcomes for Native Americans, African Americans, and whites. *Justice Quarterly,* 1994, *11,* 257-279.

Luebben, R. A. Anglo law and Navaho behavior. *The Kiva,* 1964, *29* (February), 60-75.

Lundman, R. J. Routine police arrest practices. *Social Problems,* 1974, *22,* 127-141.

MacMeekin, D. H. Red, white and Gray. *Stanford Law Review,* 1969, *21,* 1236-1248.

Petterson, J. R. Education, jurisdiction, and inadequate facilities as causes of juvenile delinquency among Indians. *North Dakota Law Review,* 1972, *48,* 661-694.

Pommersheim, F., & Wise, S. Going to the penitentiary. *Criminal Justice & Behavior,* 1989, *16,* 155-165.

Poupart, L. M. Juvenile justice precessing of American Indian youths. In K. K. Leonard, C. E. Pope & W. H. Feyerherm (Eds.), *Minorities in juvenile justice,* pp. 179-200. Thousand Oaks, CA: Sage, 1995.

Schwartz, I. M., Harris, L., & Levi, L. The jailing of juveniles in Minnesota. *Crime & Delinquency,* 1988, *34,* 133-149.

Wordes, M. , & Bynum, T. S. Policing juveniles. In K. K. Leonard, C. E. Pope & W. H. Feyerherm (Eds.), *Minorities in juvenile justice,* pp. 47-65. Thousand Oaks, CA: Sage, 1995.

Zatz, M. S., Lujan, C. C., & Snyder-Joy, Z. K. American Indians and criminal justice. In M. J. Lynch & E. B. Patterson (Eds.), *Race and criminal justice,* pp. 100-112. Albany, NY: Harrow & Heston, 1991.

Part 5

CONCLUSIONS

Chapter 16

CONCLUSIONS

The difficulties in understanding and preventing criminal behavior among Native Americans is illustrated dramatically by individual cases. For example, Rowell and Kusterer (1991) presented the case of Mark, a 34-year-old Klamath from Oregon who had been a heroin addict for fifteen years. His father was an addict and alcoholic and was killed in a fight when Mark was four. Mark's mother was also an alcoholic and abusive to her kids. Mark was sent to white fundamentalist Christian foster home when he was five, where he was also brutally beaten. He began drinking sand using drugs when he was thirteen.

Mark has a wife and two children but has been separated from them for seven years. He sends a little support now and then. His wife was an addict but stopped when she was pregnant with their second child. Mark shoots up with anyone and has unprotected sex and, so far, had refused to be tested for HIV. He has been in prison twice, for robbery and for assault.

John was born on a midwestern reservation to two alcoholic parents (Bachman, 1992). He had four older siblings, and they frequently had to hide when their drunken parents fought. He began sniffing glue at the age of eleven and drinking alcohol whenever he and his friends could get any. His parents divorced, and he lived with his mother and stepfather, but the drunkenness continued.

He began cutting school and stole his first car when he was fifteen so that he and his friends could go to the city. This led to a stay in a juvenile detention center where he began to hate whites. He returned to the reservation and began to drink heavily. He lost a job at a gasoline station through his drinking. He went back to the city and after one month was arrested for burglary after a fight with the arresting police officers. After his second release, he stayed in the city, unemployed and drinking. Six months later, he and a friend stabbed a homeowner to death while they were burglarizing his home and he came home unexpectedly.

John and his friend were drunk, and he recalled stabbing the homeowner while thinking about the system and the injustice. He ran away and obtained a gun, but was arrested before any shooting could occur. He was convicted of first-degree murder.

Jonathan, a sixteen-year-old Navajo adolescent had a complex history and set of problems (Topper, 1992). He had neurological deficits which limited his functioning. After being hospitalized at the age of two for pneumonia, he developed epilepsy. The Navajo believe that epilepsy is the result of incest which causes then to shun epileptics.

When he entered school, his intelligence was estimated to be only 70, and he had problems with visual-motor coordination. For example, he could not tie knots. In addition, he suffered from agoraphobia and psychogenic pain. When sent to an off-reservation boarding school, he became anxious and defensive when strangers were present, and he sometimes became violent under stress.

Jonathan's symptoms led his peers to ridicule him, which made him withdraw into dependence on his parents and parental surrogates. Jonathan's parents were geographically isolated and so followed the traditional Navajo way. Jonathan did not experience culture conflict until he was sent to an off-reservation boarding school where he was culturally different from his peers. Jonathan was jailed briefly on one occasion as the result of drunkenness and disorderly conduct.

What Can We Conclude?

There are three major conclusions which can be drawn from the research and commentary reviewed in this book. First, Native Americans do not have high crime rates. If we exclude those "criminal acts" which are primarily a result of public drunkenness and its subsequent effects, then Native American crime rates are extraordinary low given the socioeconomic status of Native Americans (very low) and their age structure (a high proportion of youths). The arrest rates in 1985 for violent crimes and property crimes were lower for Native Americans than for African Americans and, while higher than the arrest rates for whites, would probably not be higher were socioeconomic status and age taken into account (see Chapter 3).

Our second conclusion is that discrimination against Native Americans in the criminal justice, while it undoubtedly does occur on occasions, is not always found, and sometimes works in favor of Native Americans.

Finally, it is obvious that very little research has been conducted on Native American crime. In particular, modern theories of criminal behavior have not been explored in any great depth for their applicability to Native Americans. This omission should be rectified in the future.

Alternatives to Imprisonment

It is obvious that, since the majority of the "criminal acts" committed by Native Americans are not serious crimes, alternatives to incarceration must be found for them. Hagan (1976) noted that many Native Canadians end up in jail because they do not have the resources to pay fines. He suggested a "day-fine" system in which the amount of fine is determined by the income of the defendant. A person with an annual income of $20,000 might pay a fine of $100 whereas a person with an annual income $200,000 might pay a fine of $1,000 for the same offense. Hagan pointed out that this system cut the number of people imprisoned in Sweden for not paying fines by half.

Hagan (1976) also noted what has been obvious from this book—that the criminalization of alcohol consumption and drunkenness results in a large proportion of Native Americans in the criminal justice system. The problem is compounded by the fact that Native Americans drink and get drunk in public more while whites drink and get drunk at home more. Decriminalization of these offenses would remove the "offenders" from the criminal justice system. Furthermore, the use of community resources and detoxification centers might be less expensive than jailing, and it certainly would provide better rehabilitation services.

For Canada, Hagan (1976) estimated that decriminalization of alcohol offenses and institution of a day-fine system would reduce the number of white prisoners in Canada by 20 percent and reduce the number of Native Canadian prisoners by 51 percent.

Riffenburgh (1964) noted that restitution has a long history in many Native American tribes as a means of dealing with criminal behavior, even as serious as murder. He gave an example from the Zuni of a man who killed another and was ordered to spend half of his time tending the fields and providing for the family of the man he had killed. Hagan (1976) urged the utilization of restitution as a substitute for imprisonment for Native Canadians and suggested the following criteria for using restitution:

(1) The offense is not serious,

(2) There are resources in the community to handle restitution,

(3) Restitution is likely to be effective in preventing recidivism,

(4) The impact of arrest and imprisonment on the offender's family would be excessive relative to harm done in the criminal act, and

(5) Both the victim and offenders are agreeable to the settlement.

Finally, for those Native Americans convicted of serious crimes, better rehabilitative efforts must be made by prison systems in order to increase their chances of success upon release.

REFERENCES

Bachman, R. *Death and violence on the reservation.* New York: Auburn House, 1992.

Hagan, J. Locking up the Indians. *Canadian Forum,* 1976, *55*(2), 16-18.

Riffenburgh, A. S. Cultural influences and crime among Indian Americans of the southwest. *Federal Probation,* 1964, *28*(3), 38-46.

Rowell, R. M., & Kusterer, H. Care of HIV infected Native American substance abusers. *Journal of Chemical Dependency Treatment,* 1991, *4*(2), 91-103.

Topper, M. D. Multidimensional therapy. In L. A. Vargas & J. D. Koss-Chioino (Eds.), *Working with culture,* pp. 225-245. San Francisco: Jossey-Bass, 1992.

APPENDIX TABLES

Table 3.1
ARRESTS RATES FOR URBAN AND RURAL AREAS

	Total Arrests		Alcohol-related		Other	
	Urban	Rural	Urban	Rural	Urban	Rural
1960						
Native Americans	49,084	2,006	38,462	1,004	10,622	1,002
African Americans	7,712	991	2,568	278	5,144	713
Whites	2,101	638	1,020	224	1,081	414
Chinese/Japanese	1,256	162	308	34	948	128
1970						
Native Americans	27,535	3,593	21,069	2,131	6,467	1,462
African Americans	7,715	976	1,867	269	5,848	708
Whites	2,423	890	937	314	1.472	574
	Total		Alcohol-Related		Other	
1985						
Native-Americans	8,171		3,874		4,298	
African Americans	10,270		1,967		8,303	
whites	3,895		1,471		2,425	
Asian/Pacific Islanders	2,123		514		1,608	

From Stewart (1964), Jensen et al. (1977) and Peak and Spencer (1987).

Table 3.2
ARREST RATES BY ETHNIC GROUP*
(from Reasons [1972])

	Whites	African Americans	Native Americans	Chinese Americans	Japanese Americans
Total					
1950	572	1,957	3,492	925	261
1968	3,271	12,256	36,584	1,041	1,261
Drinking-Related					
1950	193	391	1,953	53	3
1968	1,263	3,054	27,407	216	220
Other Crimes					
1950	379	1,566	1,539	867	258
1968	2,008	9,202	9,177	825	1,041
1968					
Homicide	5	54	34		
Rape	5	45	26		
Assault	41	385	250		
Burglary	138	671	485		
Auto theft	64	341	389		
Larceny	265	1,169	913		
Robbery	19	307	149		

* rates are per 100,000 populations over the age of 14

Table 3.3
ARREST RATES PER 100,000 IN 1985*
(from Flowers, 1990)

	African Americans	Native Americans	White	Asian	Hispanic
Total crime	10273	7859	3896	2018	7604
Violent crime	763	240	117	74	333
Murder/nonneg mans	28	8	4	4	15
Forcible rape	55	17	9	5	20
Robbery	279	37	24	19	98
Aggravated assault	400	178	81	47	200
Property crime	1930	1282	607	452	1216
Burglary	416	213	141	68	316
Larceny/theft	1359	978	420	354	787
Motor vehicle theft	141	79	40	28	105
Arson	14	12	7	3	8
Other Crimes					
Fraud	347	91	102	33	73
prostitution/vice	163	33	30	32	51
drug abuse	794	217	256	121	814
driving under influence	543	1160	699	267	1237
liquor laws	223	740	208	114	237
drunkenness	541	1310	354	45	1000

Table 5.1
HOMICIDE RATES FOR NATIVE AMERICANS

	Crude rates Native American & Alaskan Native	USA	Age-adjusted rates Native American & Alaskan Native	USA
1959	14.5	4.6	20.5	5.1
1960	13.7	4.7	19.5	5.3
1961	14.7	4.7	20.9	5.3
1962	14.8	4.8	21.0	5.5
1963	16.0	4.9	22.3	5.5
1964	17.1	5.1	23.6	5.8
1965	14.7	5.5	19.7	6.3
1966	15.7	5.9	20.3	6.7
1967	15.9	6.8	20.3	7.7
1968	18.1	7.3	22.2	8.2
1969	19.4	7.7	23.4	8.6

(from Frederick, 1973; Ogden, et al., 1970)

Table 5.2
AGE-ADJUSTED HOMICIDE RATES
(from the Indian Health Service)

	Native Americans & Alaskan Natives	All USA	Nonwhites
1955	23.8	4.8	25.7
1956	21.7	5.0	26.5
1957	21.8	4.9	25.9
1958	20.4	4.9	25.3
1959	20.5	5.1	25.8
1960	19.5	5.3	25.8
1961	20.9	5.3	24.9
1962	21.0	5.5	26.3
1963	22.3	5.5	26.6
1964	23.6	5.8	27.6
1965	19.7	6.3	29.8
1966	20.3	6.7	31.9
1967	20.3	7.7	36.3
1968	22.2	8.2	38.8
1969	22.5	8.6	40.5
1970	23.8	9.1	41.3
1971	24.5	10.0	46.8
1972	23.2	10.3	46.6
1973	27.2	10.5	44.4
1974	26.4	10.8	44.5
1975	21.9	10.5	41.1
1976	21.6	9.5	36.4
1977	20.9	9.6	34.5
1978	21.2	9.6	33.4
1979	18.9	10.4	36.0
1980	18.1	10.8	35.0
1981	17.9	10.4	33.3
1982	14.9	9.7	30.0
1983	16.4	8.6	26.4
1984	14.5	8.4	24.9
1985	14.3	8.3	24.4

Table 5.3
HOMICIDE RATES BY AGE
(from the Indian Health Service)

	Native Americans 1983-1985		All USA 1984		Nonwhites 1984	
	men	*women*	*men*	*women*	*men*	*women*
0-1	11.7	4.0	7.2	5.8	17.4	13.5
1-4	5.5	1.7	2.4	2.4	4.3	5.7
5-14	1.9	0.9	1.3	1.3	2.9	2.7
15-24	28.2	7.6	18.1	5.8	52.7	13.1
25-34	41.3	13.2	23.5	5.9	78.4	16.4
35-44	32.6	9.5	18.2	4.7	62.8	12.4
45-54	27.8	12.5	14.1	3.3	47.4	7.2
55-65	20.9	4.1	9.4	2.6	35.0	6.0
65-74	18.5	6.9	6.5	2.3	26.6	6.1
75-84	18.6	2.9	6.2	3.4	24.9	8.5
85+	-	9.5	7.3	3.1	25.7	8.7

Table 14.1
RATE OF INCARCERATION PER 100,000 IN 1983
(from Flowers, 1990)

	Native American	*African American*	*White*	*Hispanic*	*Asian*
federal	46	39	11	51	6
state	242	716	109	230	40

AUTHOR INDEX

A

Aalberg, V., 12
Aase, J. M., 217
Ackerman, L. A., 89, 95
Akers, R. L., 111, 120
Alexander, R., 31, 39
Alvarez, A., 160, 167
Armstrong, T. L., 29, 38
Asu, M. E., 101
Austin, W. T., 34, 38, 45, 49

B

Bachman, R., 53, 56, 60, 63, 160, 167,
  171, 174
Back, W. D., 44, 49
Baffi, C. R., 16, 22
Bahr, H. M., 39, 40, 96, 138, 154, 167
Baker, J. L., 56, 63
Baker, S. P., 152
Bakkestrom, E., 101
Bandura, A., 111, 120
Barker, M. L., 129, 131
Barnes, G., 22
Barsh, R. L., 124, 131
Beauvais, F., 49
Beccaria, C., 91, 95
Bechtold, D., W. 76
Becker, H., 117, 120
Becker, T. M., 22, 64
Benjamin, R., 141, 152, 162, 167
Bennison, L., 99, 100
Bentham, J., 91, 95
Berg, G., 20
Bergeisen, L., 76
Berlin, I. N., 75, 76
Bienvenue, P. M., 164, 167
Biernoff, M. P., 76

Bird, M. E., 76
Bjorntorp, P., 21
Blum, R. W., 70, 76
Blyan, J. D., 152
Boldt, E. D., 131, 164
Boldt, M., 14, 21, 54, 64, 167
Bollinger, J., 21
Bond-Maupin, L. J., 149, 150, 152
Bonta, J., 166, 167
Bortner, M. A., 152
Brakel, S. J., 135, 138
Brantner, J., 58, 65
Bratude, A. P., 50
Brenneman, G., 64
Brodoff, B. N., 21
Brodribb, S., 79, 83
Brooks, J. H., 98, 100
Brown, E. M., 50
Bruneau, O. J., 99, 100
Buffler, P., 54, 64
Bynum, T. S., 156, 161, 167, 168

C

Carman, R. S., 21
Carter, I., 69, 76
Caulkins, D., 81, 83
Chadwick, B. A., 39, 40, 96, 136, 138,
  167
Chester, B., 77
Christiansen, K. O., 98, 100, 101
Cloward, R., 105, 108
Cohen, A., 104, 108
Cohen, F. G., 45, 49
Copus, G., 127, 131
Cornell, S., 18, 20
Cornely, D A., 66, 73, 77

Cortes, J. B., 98, 100
Cozzetto, D. A., 19, 20
Craig, B. H. R., 21, 76
Cranston, V. A., 32, 38
Cressey, D., 111, 120
Cross, S., 21
Cummings, M., 21

D

Daniels, H. W., 152
Danto, B. L., 145, 152
Danziger, S. H., 17, 20
Day, R. C., 39, 96, 138
De Witt, D. C., 81, 83
DeBruyn, L. M., 74, 76
Decker, J., 152
Delk, J. L., 16, 20
Deloria, V., 135, 138
Dietrich, G., 66, 76
Dobrec, A., 131
Dobyns, H. F., 6, 12
Dodder, R. A., 43, 49
Doraz, W., 98, 101
Doyle-Martin, S. M., 157, 167
Duclos, C. W., 142, 144, 145, 146, 152
Dumoff, R., 22
Durst, D., 80, 83

E

Edwards, R., 21, 49, 83
Eiskovitz, Z., 39
Elia, C., 19, 20
Elias, G. L., 152
Ellis, L., 99, 100
Empey, L., 96
Emrich, L. J., 21
Evans, A. L., 12
Everett, M. W., 62, 63, 147, 152
Eysenck, H. J., 99, 101

F

Farber, W. O., 23, 28
Favazza, A., R. 64
Feimer, S., 163, 167, 168
Feinman, C., 78, 83, 125, 131

Feit, M., 152
Feld, B. C., 161, 167
Ferguson, F. N., 41, 47, 49
Ferracuti, F., 103, 108
Ferri, E., 97
Feyerherm, W. H., 167, 168
Fischer, M., 69, 76
Fischler, R. S., 66, 75, 76
Fisher, G. A., 157, 167
Fishman, G., 39
Fitzgerald, B. J., 21
Flaherty, M. G., 145, 152
Flowers, R. B., 26, 38, 80, 83, 88, 89, 90,
    95, 140, 152, 178, 181
Flynn, F., 64
Forquera, R., 21
Forslund, M. A., 16, 20, 21, 32, 37, 38
Foulks, E. F., 64
Fox, J., 12
Frederick, C. J., 53, 63, 179
French, L. A., 38, 48, 49, 56, 58, 59, 64,
    65, 69, 76, 82, 83, 147
Frideres, J. S., 5, 12, 31, 38

G

Galaway, B., 135, 138, 139
Garbarino, M. S., 90, 95
Garcia-Mason, V., 21, 83
Garofalo, R., 97, 101
Gatti, F. M., 98, 100
Goldman, D., 77
Goldstein, G. S., 15, 21, 82, 83
Goldstone, C. S., 87, 96
Goodenough, D., 101
Goodwin, C., 64
Goring, C., 97, 101
Graves, T. D., 33, 38, 39
Green, B. E., 19, 21
Griffiths, C. T., 87, 96, 120, 128, 131
Grobsmith, E. S., 46, 49, 140, 147, 152
Grossman, D. C., 13, 21
Grossman, M. G., 146, 152
Guilfoyle, M. H., 38
Gundlach, J. H., 7, 12, 19, 21
Gustavsson, N. S., 21

Guttman, E., 39

H

Hagan, J., 161, 165, 167, 173, 174
Hall, E., 118, 120, 155, 158, 167
Halverson, L. K., 137, 138
Handler, A., 64
Hanson, R. C., 39
Harlan, J. R., 159, 167
Harman, B., 76
Harring, S., 24, 26, 38
Harris, L., 39, 76, 168
Harris, V. W., 39
Harrison, G. G., 17, 21
Harrison, W., 95
Hartnagel, T. F., 157, 167
Hayner, N., 105, 108
Helgerson, S. D., 22
Henderson, J. Y., 124, 131
Hiat, A. B., 76
Hill, C. A., 64
Hindelang, M., 99, 101
Hirschhorn, K., 101
Hirschi, T., 99, 101, 112, 120
Holmgren, C., 15, 21
Holscher, L. M., 147, 152
Honigmann, I., 41, 49
Honigmann, J. J., 41, 49
Hood, D. L., 159, 167
Horejsi, C., 15, 21, 74, 75, 76
Hornbuckle, J., 56, 64
Hovens, P., 30, 39
Howard, J. H., 81, 83
Howard, V. F., 21
Howitt, R., 101
Hudson, J., 135, 138, 139
Hughes, S. P., 43, 49
Hull, G. H., 66, 74, 76
Humphrey, G. W., 149, 152
Humphrey, J. A., 57, 64
Hunter, D. K., 39
Hursh, L. E., 167
Hutchings, M., 98, 101
Hutton, C., 165, 168
Hymbaugh, K. J., 21

I

Inui, I. S., 106, 108
Ivy, S. C., 25, 39

J

Jacobs, D. F., 19, 20
Jaranson, J. M., 77
Jarvis, G. K., 14, 21, 54, 64
Jensen, G. F., 25, 31, 37, 39, 176
Jessor, R., 23, 39
Jessor, S. L., 39
Jilek, W., 54, 57, 64
Jilek-Aall, L., 55, 64
Joe, K., 39
Johnson, B. B., 19, 21
Johnson, S. D., 167

K

Kahn, M. W., 20
Kalt, J. P., 18, 20
Kane, R., 73, 76
Kempe, H., 77
Key, C. R., 22, 64
Kim, C. N., 141, 152, 162, 167
Kirmayer, L., 9, 12
Koss-Chioino, J. D., 131, 174
Kraus, R., 54, 64
Krieger, J. W., 21
Krisberg, B., 23, 39
Kroeber, A. L., 6, 12
Kunitz, S. J., 16, 21, 37, 54, 61, 64, 119, 120
Kupferer, H. J., 57, 64
Kusterer, H., 71, 77, 171, 174

L

Lane, E. B., 100, 101, 141, 152
Lane, J. M., 77
LaPlante, C., 50, 139, 153
LaPrairie, C. P., 30, 39, 88, 95, 107, 108, 142, 152
Latif, A. H., 164, 167
Laub, J., 32, 39
LeBeau, W., 152
Leiber, M. J., 163, 168

Lemert, E., 117, 118, 120
Leonard, K. K., 167, 168
Lesieur, H. R., 20, 21
Lester, D., 11, 12, 59, 60, 64, 100, 101, 103, 145, 152
Levi, L., 39, 168
Levy, J. E., 11, 12, 21, 37, 54, 56, 61, 64, 118, 119, 120
Lewis, A., 21
Lewis, C., 81, 83
Lewis, R., 152
Li, T. K., 99, 100
Lin, R. L., 159, 167
Lombroso, C., 92
Long, K. A., 67, 76
Luebben, R. A., 155, 168
Lujan, C. C., 29, 39, 55, 64, 72, 76, 152, 168
Lundman, R. J., 156, 168
Lundsteen, C., 101
Lyle, J., 64
Lynch, M. J., 168
Lytle, C. M., 135, 138

M
MacEachron, A. E., 18, 21
MacMeekin, D. H., 165, 168
Maguire, K., 28, 39
Mahoney, M. C., 13, 21
Mandelzys, N., 100, 101
Mann, C. R., 26, 27, 39, 83, 138, 148, 152
Mannheim, H., 101
Manson, S. M., 76, 78, 83
Marenin, O., 127, 131
Marshall, D. L., 62, 64
Martin, M. D., 143, 152
Matza, D., 110, 120
May, P. A., 15, 17, 21, 44, 49, 53, 64, 76, 87, 85
McBeth, S. J., 19, 21
McCandless, B. R., 98, 101
McCone, C. R., 23, 39
McKay, H. D., 102, 108
McLaughlin, T. F., 16, 21

Mednick, S. A., 98, 100, 101
Melton, P., 38
Merriam, L., 19, 21
Merton, R., 104, 108
Messerschmidt, J., 83
Meyers, R. E., 37, 38
Michalek, A. M., 21
Mikel, D., 7, 12, 30, 39
Miller, F., 81, 83
Miller, R., 101
Miller, W., 103, 108
Mills, D. K., 36, 39, 150, 152
Minnis, M. S., 89, 90, 96, 105, 108
Moffatt, E. K., 22
Molesworth, C., 39
Montaigne, F. , 18, 22, 41, 49, 80, 83
Mullen, K., 129, 131
Murray, C., 98, 101

N
Nagi, S. Z., 71, 76
Nasca, P. C., 21
Nash, D. R., 124, 129, 131
Neider, J., 47, 50
Neilsen, M. O., 38, 39, 136, 167
Newman, G., 92, 96
Norgren, J., 132, 138
Norton, I. M., 78, 83
Nuffield, J., 87, 96
Nurge, E., 84
Nyborg, H., 99, 100

O
O'Brien, M. J., 35, 39
O'Neill, J. D., 22
Oakland, L., 73, 76
Odeen, P. A., 38
Odoroff, C. L., 21
Oetting, E. R., 21, 42, 49, 83
Ogden, M., 53, 64, 179
Oge, L., 22
Ohlin, L., 105, 108
Olsen, L. K., 16, 22
Olson, L. M., 14, 22, 55, 64
Owen, D., 101

P

Pablo, J., 21, 76
Pambrum, A., 21
Paolucci, H., 95
Paredes, A., 50
Parker, L. J., 69, 76
Pastore, A. L., 28, 39
Paternoster, R., 161, 167
Patterson, E. B., 168
Patton, M. Q., 76
Peak, K., 26, 27, 39, 123, 131, 132, 138, 148, 152, 176
Peake, E., 80, 84
Perkins, C., 167
Persons, W. S., 101
Petterson, J. R., 88, 89, 90, 96, 155, 168
Philip, J., 101
Phillips, M. R., 106, 108
Piasecki, J. M., 72, 76
Pommersheim, F., 164, 167, 168
Pope, C. E., 167, 168
Poupart, L. M., 160, 168
Price, J., 81, 84

Q

Quinney, R., 95, 96

R

Raboin, R., M. 20
Randall, A., 45, 49, 82, 96
Randall, B., 45, 49, 87, 96
Rasmussen, J. K., 77
Reasons, C., 25, 39, 88, 90, 96, 151, 152, 177
Reckless, W., 114, 120
Red Horse, J. G., 151, 152
Reddon, J. R., 98, 100, 101
Reed, L. R., 148, 152
Reid, P. N., 12, 21
Reid, R., 152
Resnick, M. D., 76
Reyes, R., 21
Rhoades, E. R., 55, 64
Riffenburgh, A. S., 46, 49, 81, 84, 173, 174

Ritenbaugh, C. K., 17, 21
Robbins, S. P., 31, 39, 114, 115, 120
Robbins, W., 50, 139, 153
Roberts, A., 12, 21, 101
Roberts, L. W., 131
Robertson, B., 5, 12, 31, 38
Robin, R. W., 70, 77
Rowell, R. M., 71, 77, 171, 174
Roy, C., 54, 57, 64
Royer, R., 152
Rubin, D., 101

S

Sack, W. H., 21
Sakamoto, A., 18, 22
Samet, J. M., 21, 22, 64
Sandefur, G. D., 7, 12, 17, 18, 20, 21
Satchell, M., 7, 12
Schoenfeldt, L. F., 22
Schoenthaler, S., 98, 101
Schulsinger, F., 101
Schur, E., 117, 120
Schwartz, I., 23, 39, 157, 168
Schwendinger, H., 95, 96
Schwendinger, J., 95, 96
Sellers, C. S., 120
Sellin, T., 97, 101, 103, 108
Shattuck, P. T., 132, 138
Shaw, C. R., 102, 108
Sheldon, W. H., 98, 101
Shepardson, M., 134, 138
Silverman, R. A., 28, 38, 39, 167
Siminoski, K. G., 101
Simkus, A., 118, 120, 155, 158, 167
Simmons, J. L., 9, 12
Simpson, S. G., 146, 152
Sims, O. S., 22
Skoog, D., 128, 131
Smart, R. G., 44, 49
Smith, M. B., 44, 49
Snipes, D. S. B., 131
Snipp, C. M., 6, 12
Snyder-Joy, Z. K., 168
Sorkin, A. L., 33, 39
Soule, S., 62, 64

Spector, M. I., 64
Spencer, J., 26, 39
Stanley, S., 49
Stauss, J. H., 39, 138, 167
Stewart, O., 24, 39, 176
Stocking, M., 101
Stratton, J., 42, 50
Stratton, R., 41, 50
Strimbu, J. L., 15, 22
Stuart, B., 136, 138
Studer, L. H., 99, 101
Stuler, H., 39
Sugarman, J. R., 14, 21, 22
Sullivan, D. A., 14, 22
Sutherland, E. H., 109, 111, 120
Swanson, D. W., 42, 50
Sykes, G., 95, 96, 110, 120

T

Taylor, K. W., 167
Taylor, S. S., 76
Teret, S., 152
Thompson, S. D.,147, 153
Thornton, R., 6, 8, 9, 12
Thunderhorse, I., 149, 153
Toch, H., 99, 101
Topper, M. D., 173, 174
Tousey, T. F., 81, 84
Trott, L., 16, 22
Trovato, F., 14, 22
Tschetter, R. A., 38
Tso, T., 134, 138
Tyler, I. M., 147, 153

U

Unger, S., 21
Urbancik, G., 30

V

Valliant, P. M., 100, 101
Vargas, L. A., 131, 174
Vold, G. B., 91, 95, 96
Von Hentig, H., 23, 40
Von Hirsch, A., 92, 96

W

Wachtel, D., 123, 125, 126, 127, 131
Waddell, J. O., 38, 45, 50, 95
Walker, R. D., 49
Ward, J. A., 9, 12
Warren, C. W., 22
Watson, O. M., 38, 95
Wechsler, J. G., 68, 77
Weibel-Orlando, J., 44, 50
Weinberg, D. H., 20
Westermeyer, J., 47, 50, 58, 64, 65, 80
White, R. A., 81, 84
White, R. B., 66, 73, 77
Whittaker, J. O., 44, 50
Wichlacz, C. R., 68, 71, 77
Wiggins, C. L., 22, 64
Williams, B. F., 21
Williams, C., 20
Williams, D., 98, 101
Williams, L. E., 34, 40
Williams, T. R., 63
Willis, D. J., 130, 131
Winfree, T. L., 87, 96, 111, 120
Wintrob, R. M., 64
Wise, S., 164, 167, 168
Witkin, H., 98, 101
Wolff, P. H., 99, 101
Wolfgang, M. E., 97, 101, 103, 108
Wordes, M., 156, 168
Wormith, J. S., 87, 96

Y

Yazzi, R., 136, 139
Yerbury, J. C., 128, 131
Young, T. J., 11, 12, 15, 22, 48, 50, 58, 65,
    126, 131, 133, 139, 148, 153
Young, T. K., 14, 22

Z

Zatz, M. S., 157, 168
Zeiner, A., 50
Zion, J. W., 136, 139

SUBJECT INDEX

A

Aborigines, 5
Acculturation, 62, 88, 107
Adoption, 18
Alaska, 127
Alaskan Natives, 13, 54, 62, 69, 70, 106
Alcohol abuse, 10, 15, 18, 19, 42, 55, 73, 75, 90, 111, 126, 140, 150
Alcohol and crime, 41
Alcohol-related offenses, 23
Alcoholics Anonymous, 47
Aleut, 54, 106, 127
American Association for Indian Affairs, 61
American Indian Movement, 83, 126
American Indian Religious Freedom Act, 147
Anomie, 90
Apache, 16, 17, 18, 26, 37, 54, 61, 62, 63, 123, 147
Arapaho, 6, 36
Arrest rates, 24
Arrests and discrimination, 155
Asian roots, 5
Athabascans, 54
Australia, 5

B

Birth rate, 8
Blackfoot, 61
Boarding schools, 19, 74, 79, 88
Bootlegging, 45, 126, 155
Bureau of Indian Affairs, 5, 7, 19, 33, 69, 100, 107, 123, 124, 129, 130, 134, 143, 145, 150

C

Canada, 5, 9, 14, 16, 30, 44, 54, 79, 81, 87, 98, 99, 128, 136, 141, 146, 155, 157, 161, 164, 165, 166, 173, 174
Casinos, 7
Cherokee, 6, 7, 8, 41, 56, 57
Cheyenne, 61
Cheyenne River Siouz Indian Reservation, 71, 148
Cheyenne/Arapaho, 41
Child abuse, 66, 140
Child sexual abuse, 69
Chippewa, 58, 69, 148
Cirrhosis, 13, 16, 62
Classical theories, 91
Comanche, 61
Containment theory, 114
Courts, 132
Cree, 99
Crow, 45, 61, 71
Culture deviance theory, 102

D

Dawes Act, 7
Death rate, 8, 14
Diet, 98
Differential association theory, 109
Discrimination, 116, 154
Doukhobor, 55
Drift theory, 110
Drug abuse, 15
Drug Enforcement Administration, 82
Drug offenses, 82
Drunkenness, 16, 45

E

Eskimo, 10, 54, 106, 127

F

Federal Bureau of Investigation, 53, 82, 83, 130
Fetal alcohol syndrome, 16
Firearms, 56
Fort Hall Indian Reservation, 105
Frequency of crime, 23

G

Gambling, 19, 82
Gangs, 81
General Crimes Act, 132
Genes, 97
Genocide, 6, 29
Geronimo, 123
Gray v United States, 165

H

Health, 13
Hopi, 16, 37, 61, 118, 133, 146

I

Incest, 69
Indian Child Welfare Act, 18, 66, 67
Indian Civil Rights Act, 123
Indian Health Service, 5, 53, 58, 67, 180, 181
Indian Removal Act, 6, 132
Indian Vocational Training Act, 33
Indian Youth of America, 163
Infant mortality, 8, 13, 14
Inhalants, 15, 42, 46, 140
International Association of Chiefs of Police, 129
Inuit, 10
Iowa, 123
Iroquois, 6

J

Juvenile delinquency, 29, 35, 42, 111

K

Kiowa, 61
Klamath, 71, 105, 171

L

Labeling theory, 116
Lakota, 133
Law, 165
Law Enforcement Association Administration, 127
Learning theory, 109
Legal services, 90, 136
Lumbee, 57

M

Mafia, 81
Marijuana, 15, 32, 42, 111
Mennonites, 55
Menominee Indian Reservation, 81
Métis, 10
Minnesota Anishinabe Longhouse, 148
MMPI, 100
Murder, 13, 25, 26, 27, 30, 44, 53, 106 146, 147, 160, 161, 172, 174
Murder victims, 56
Murderers, 56

N

Native American Rights Fund, 48, 133, 148
Navajo, 16, 17, 33, 37, 42, 53, 56, 61, 73, 78, 81, 82, 123, 124, 133, 134, 147, 155, 172
Nebraska Consent Decree 147
Nez Perces, 89
Neutralization theory, 110

O

Obesity, 17
Oil, 133
Oliphant v Squamish, 124
Omaha, 142, 148
Omnibus Crime Control & Safe Streets Act, 127
OPEC, 133

Oppression, 5, 66, 75, 93, 124
Organized crime, 82

P

Paiute, 61
Papago, 16, 45
Parole, 141, 150
Peltier, Leonard 83
Physiological theories, 97
Physique, 98
Pima, 17
Pine Ridge Indian Reservation, 81
Plea negotiation, 157
Police, 31, 42, 89, 107, 154
Police encounters, 156
Policing, 123
Political prisoners, 82
Pomo, 71
Ponca, 148
Positivist theories, 97
Poverty, 7, 17, 74, 90, 105
Prison, 46, 140, 166
Prisoners, 25, 29
Probation, 150, 155
Prohibition, 35, 44, 90, 123, 126, 132, 156
Psychiatric disorder, 19
Public Law #, 280 129
Pueblo, 17, 26, 61, 72, 133

R

Racial discrimination, 89
Recidivism, 87
Religious freedom, 147
Religious practices, 48
Relocation, 6, 19
Relocation Act, 133
Reservations, 6
Restitution, 174
Restorative justice, 135

S

Sac-Fox, 123
Salish, 55
San Carlos Apache Reservation, 123

Self-reported crime rate, 31
Seminole, 6, 31, 114
Seneca, 6, 13
Sentencing, 158
Sexual abuse, 146
Shoshone (Shoshoni), 6, 36, 61
Shoshone/Arapahoe, 15
Shoshoni/Bannock, 11, 105, 118
Sioux, 7, 18, 61, 69, 148
Soboba, 133
Social bond theory, 112
Social conflict theories, 92
Social control theory, 112
Social disorganization, 88
Social integration, 61
Social process theory, 109
Social reaction theory, 116
Social structure theory, 102, 105
Spouse abuse, 78
Standing Rock Indian Reservation, 17, 41, 80
Stigma, 116
Strain theory, 104
Subcultures, 110
Suicide, 11, 44, 54, 57, 58, 59, 62
Suicide in prison, 144
Sweatlodge, 47, 48, 141, 148
Swift Bird Project, 148

T

Testosterone, 98
Thunderbird Prison Alliance, 149
Toxic waste dumping, 81
Tribal courts, 134, 143
Tribal law, 68
Tribal police, 45

U

Umatilla Indian Reservation, 129
United States v Switzler, 35
Urban/rural, 14, 24, 32, 33, 81, 107, 115, 142, 161
Urbanization, 9
Ute, 17

V

Victimization, 80

W

Warfare, 6
Warm Springs Indian Reservation, 35
Water rights, 133
White collar crime, 80

Wikwemikong Indian Reservation, 10
Wind River Indian Reservation, 6, 36
Winnebago, 148
Women, 29, 55, 142, 146, 165

Z

Zuni, 174